Intelligence + Character,
Is the True Goal of
Education by *Dr. M.L. King Jr.*

The Power of Living Raw
Delicious and flavourful recipes for health and wellbeing

NICKY ARTHUR

D0910593

Dedication

I dedicate this book to my girls, Lucia my spiritual light, and Millijana my energizing pocket rocket. Health and happiness is everything to me. I continually strive to provide my girls with a depth of knowledge about healthy living, teaching them how to have a positive mindset and about the benefits of making a difference to our universe. It means the world o know that they are growing up with such a holistic, unique and loving way of life.

To my amazing support team: Lucia and Millijana, Mum, Dad, Aunty Marlene, Janine, Jeff, Audrey, Gav, Jacinda, Christina, Kim, Sage, Marayke and John, and my Bikram Bestie Tina; you guys are always at the top of my daily gratitude list. Dad, I can't express how much I value the way that you and Mum provided me with a simple and unfussy way of life.

A message: Hi, I am Millijana, Nicky Arthur's daughter, and I am eight years old, I am very active and I love my mummy when she makes me those yummy **Raw** healthy ice creams.

What a focused and conscious mind can create, a balanced and energized soul can deliver.

Nicky Arthur

The Power of Living Raw

Delicious and flavourful recipes for health and wellbeing

NICKY ARTHUR

First published in 2014 by
New Holland Publishers
London • Sydney • Auckland
www.newhollandpublishers.com • www.newholland.com.au

The Chandlery Unit 114 50 Westminster Bridge Road London SE1 7QY
1/66 Gibbes Street Chatswood NSW 2067 Australia
218 Lake Road Northcote Auckland New Zealand

A catalogue record of this book is available at the British Library and at the National Library of Australia

ISBN: 9781742575421

10 9 8 7 6 5 4 3 2 1

Managing Director: Fiona Schultz
Publisher: Linda Williams
Editor: Simona Hill
Designer: Caryanne Cleevely
Stylist: Aimee Jones
Photographer: Sue Stubbs
Production director: Olga Dementiev
Printer: Toppan Leefung Printing Limited

Follow New Holland Publishers on
Facebook: www.facebook.com/NewHollandPublishers

Contents

Introduction

I started my **Raw** food journey more than four years ago and the difference in how I feel has completely transformed my body, life and mind.

Since stepping outside my comfort zone and embracing a more creative style of food preparation, I've come to enjoy and appreciate natural food and its awesome healing power. **Raw** food gives my body unlimited energy, generating happiness that I am blessed to experience. I feel transformed and I want to share the benefits that I enjoy with you.

Today's world has become so busy that we often don't realise that we are not looking after our body and digestive system as best as we can. I believe that it is critical to listen to our body and to learn how to feed ourself in a way that nurtures both body and mind, restores our equilibrium and rejuvenates us, so that we benefit from optimum health.

The recipes that I provide in this book have been designed to accelerate your energy levels and to promote your sense of wellbeing, so that you have the energy to create a healthy, balanced lifestyle and live your busy life.

Raw Food Benefits

I believe that taking care of yourself is the best insurance that you can have for a vibrant life full of joy and happiness, and that eating a good diet, rich in vitamins and minerals, will help to promote good health.

For me, a **Raw** food lifestyle begins with reassessing the basic foods provided for us by nature. In order to do that, I believe that it is essential to strip out of our diets all foods that are processed or packaged, loaded with artificial flavour enhancers and sweeteners and which are devoid of nutritional value.

Nature provides us with a whole array of healthy foods, which, when incorporated into our diet, provides us with vitality, good health and energy. These foods can offer a perfect nutritional package. When eaten **Raw**, we benefit from the maximum nutritional value that each of these foods offers.

I believe that 'living' foods – meaning those that grow in the ground – are our life force. By integrating living foods into our diets, we can look forward to wellness, greater energy, mental clarity, a positive outlook on life and spiritual awakening.

When you eat **Raw** food, you'll notice that you don't need to eat so much, or need to eat the heavier foods that you previously desired. Lighter food makes us feel lighter and more energized. You'll never feel as if you are on a diet when eating this way.

What Are Raw Foods?

Living foods are plant-based foods to be eaten in their original, or **Raw**, uncooked state. They are alive, pulsing with energy and life force. When eaten **Raw**, or prepared in a dehydrator at less than 48°C/118°F, they retain their vital life force. They are easy for our body to process and break down, and may help to protect us from ill health.

Raw foods include fruits, vegetables, grains, nuts, seeds, seaweed and fresh juices. We also need **Raw** cold-pressed oils and fats in the diet to help produce hormones and to maintain a healthy nervous system. We benefit from eating foods plentiful in omegas 3, 6 and 9, including green vegetables nuts and seeds. These foods deliver an abundance of nutrients that the body requires to promote a healthy digestive system, optimal joint health, improved brain function, muscle repair and longevity.

Raw Food Lifestyle Tips

Our health can be affected by poor nutrition – specifically poor food choices – as well as too much stress in our lives and an unhealthy environment.

When we eat processed, high sugar, overcooked foods and too much meat, the body is thrown out of balance. For some people, this can result in a range of symptoms such as sugar cravings, chronic fatigue, digestive disorders and even eating disorders.

In contrast, **Raw** food is the ultimate nutrition plan and a **Raw** food-based lifestyle is healthy for the body. As you learn to eat a wider variety of **Raw** foods, you will start to benefit from the broad array of vitamins, minerals and trace elements found in those foods that are essential for health and vitality. The enzymes in **Raw** foods also make their digestion so much easier, allowing the body to use more energy to perform other functions.

Living a **Raw** food lifestyle doesn't necessarily mean you have to eat 100 per cent of your food **Raw**. In my recipes, most of the food I make is eaten **Raw**, and I encourage you to take 80 per cent of the food that you eat **Raw** and cook only 20 per cent of it. You will notice a huge difference in how you feel even with smaller, more gradual increases in your **Raw** food intake.

Organic Raw Foods

I always choose organic produce whenever I can. From personal experience of living a busy lifestyle, I realise that sourcing organic produce can be a challenge. Often we grab food on the run, seizing what's convenient when we are most hungry. If you cannot regularly eat organic food, try to look for pesticide-free produce.

Mindfulness

Practising mindfulness toward food can help manage stress and improve digestion. Breathing before you eat and eating slowly, without rushing your food, can make a big difference. Additionally making sure that you are not emotional or stressed when you eat can be helpful for healthy digestion, vitality and longevity.

Yoga

The **Raw** food lifestyle can bring even more benefits if you combine it with the daily practice of yoga or meditation. Daily practice can help you to become more connected to what feels natural and intuitive for your body and more able to listen to your body's needs.

Practising meditation can help to minimise stress, while yoga can help to cleanse and purify the internal body, including the digestive system. When I started my own yoga studies and practice, I began to learn how yoga can improve the body's internal health. When you are in a yoga posture, you are temporarily cutting off the blood flow to certain internal organs. When you release out of the posture, fresh blood surges back and massages your organs, bringing nourishment to every blood cell and muscle in your body, from the inside out.

Yoga can also enhance your **Raw** food journey by helping to balance food cravings. Over time, you will notice that you no longer look for alcohol, sugar or chocolate to please you. You will enjoy more sustained energy and experience less mood swings, less low moods, less sadness, anger and frustration.

Gardening and Raw Foods

I was blessed to grow up around nature. When I was a child, my Dad started an amazing vegetable garden that he still harvests produce from today.

Many years later, I am able to look back and truly appreciate my childhood days in Dad's colourful, lush garden. I clearly remember the apple trees in the back garden, the compost, the well cared for green grass and the delicious variety of living food that we enjoyed from the garden each season.

After school we always seemed to be playing outside in the garden, never inside, and we rarely watched television. In those days, of course, we didn't have laptops or mobile phones. Instead, I have memories of often sitting and helping Dad to pod peas and scrub the rich dark earth from the organic potatoes. We also picked beautiful big runner beans and broad beans, as well as fresh baby carrots.

Even now, I can remember the sour taste of the crunchy small apples from our garden and the particularly vivid taste of the gooseberries from the garden of our dear next door neighbour, Nana Barnes. And, I remember the pleasure of eating the different varieties of fruit and vegetables that were naturally harvested in different seasons.

Children love connecting to nature and Dad's lush garden is now something that I can share with my children. My girls love running around outside. Being around nature is stress free and an opportunity for my family to connect with the earth and its bounty. It's educational too: an opportunity, for example, to learn that worms are an important part of the gardening process.

In my childhood memories, Dad often talked about his soil; it was 'the best soil'. I still hold vivid memories of Dad running the dark soil through his hands. Dad also follows good gardening practise that is in alignment with nature, such as saving the seeds from this year's produce and storing them for later sowings.

Community Gardening

I learned from Dad that gardens take passion and time. Now that I have a family of my own, I have the passion for a great garden, but not always the time. So I've joined a community garden. In a community garden, I can teach my girls the importance of nature and the pleasure of gardening. They also learn to connect food with where it comes from and why and how to eat in season. They learn some of the same skills that I were passed to me from Dad, including how to make compost and how to plant seeds.

Seasonal Eating

Imagine a vegetable garden in the dead of winter. Then imagine the same garden on a sunny, summer day. How different the garden is during these two seasons of the year! Yet, today it is so easy for us to forget about the seasons when we eat.

Originally, people had no choice but to eat foods only when they were in season. But now, modern food propagation methods and a fast and economical worldwide distribution of food make the same foods available all year round. You can buy many types of food from a supermarket irrespective of seasonal availability, and grocery store shelves look much the same in December as they do in July.

However, life always comes full circle and now, once again, we are moving back to the old approach of following the seasons. Seasonal foods are a way of reconnecting with the cycle that nature intended for us. **Raw** foods, the healthiest wholesome foods provided by nature, are seasonal. And when food is in season, it has more flavour and is more economical to buy.

Freshness

The nutritional level of fresh, seasonal food is very high. The longer that it is stored the more the nutritional value depletes. So, it's a good idea to eat freshly picked fruit, or freshly harvested produce. Try supporting your local farmers' market or your local fresh fruit and vegetable store, because generally they will stock what is in season.

What Does Seasonal Eating Mean?

I align what I eat as closely to nature as possible. I believe that our bodies will get different nutrients, minerals and vitamins from what may be in season today than from what will be in season in a few months' time. Seasonal eating helps us to benefit from a wide variety of nutrients throughout the year and to enjoy optimal health. It also ensures that we do not overdose on any one food.

To enjoy the full nourishment of food, you must make your menu a seasonal one. In different parts of the world, and even in different regions of one country, seasonal menus can vary. But here are some overriding principles you can follow to ensure optimal nourishment in every season:

In spring, focus on tender, leafy vegetables that represent the fresh new growth of the season. The greening that occurs in springtime should be represented by greens on your plate, including spinach, lettuce, basil and parsley.

In the hot days of summer, stick with traditionally light, cooling foods. These foods include broccoli and cauliflower and fruits such as apple, pear, strawberry and plum.

In autumn, turn toward the more filling root vegetable crops such as potato, carrots, onion and garlic. Emphasize the warming spices such as ginger, cayenne, peppercorns and turmeric in your diet.

In winter, turn even more exclusively toward warming foods. Remember the principle that foods that take longer to grow are generally more warming than foods that grow quickly. Root vegetables such as sweet potato and carrot, as well as onions, garlic, corn and nuts also fit here.

Final Words

My purpose in writing this book is to help you transform to a lifestyle that provides you with a healthy life, a pain-free body, contentment and longevity. On my **Raw** food journey, I have learned new ways of creating healthy food that serves my body well and keeps me healthy. Life comes with choices, and you can choose **Raw** food healthy eating to become part of your life.

Be mindful of the foods that you put into your body. Make peace with your body and nurture it with the food it needs.

Essential Raw Ingredients

All of the ingredients below are used in the recipes within this book. Incorporating them into your diet will promote good health.

Vegetables and Salad Vegetables

Avocado
High in essential and healthy fats, a great food for brain function, very low in cholesterol and sodium. It is also a good source of dietary fibre, vitamins C and K and folate. Avocado is a natural healthy food with high nutritional value.

Bell Pepper (Capsicum)
Bell peppers are a great, low calorie snack. They contain very high amounts of vitamins A and C. Bell peppers also contain significant amounts of vitamin B6 and dietary fibre.

Beetroot (Beets)
An excellent source of folate and manganese. Beetroot, with its vibrant pigment is high in phytochemicals and anti-oxidants that help protect the body's cells from damage by free radicals. An anti-inflammatory that provides detoxification support.

Broccoli
High in anti-oxidants and healing powers, broccoli contains vitamins A, B1, B2, B3, B5, B6, B9 and C. Broccoli contains calcium, iron, magnesium, phosphorus, potassium and zinc. These vitamins and minerals aren't just found in tiny trace amounts either. For example, ounce for ounce, broccoli contains more vitamin C than many citrus fruits, is higher in calcium than milk, and will provide more fibre that grainy bread.

Cabbage
Cabbage is an excellent source of manganese, potassium, calcium, iron, phosphorous and magnesium. It contains high levels of fibre, folate, omega-3 fatty acids, zinc, sodium and copper. The only downside is that over-consumption can cause gas. Like all vegetables, cabbage is low in calories, a great weight-loss food, an anti-inflammatory, and beneficial for peptic ulcers. High in vitamin C, it is a great winter food that helps protect from the damage caused by free radicals.

Carrots

Carrots provide the body with many essential vitamins and minerals including vitamins A, B1, B3, B6 C and K, potassium, manganese, phosphorous, magnesium and folate and they are a good source of dietary fibre. Carrots are the greatest vegetable source of pro-vitamin A carotene. The powerful anti-oxidants found in carrots help protect the body from cardiovascular disease, as well as cancer, and they're also great for promoting good vision due to the high levels of beta-carotene (which is converted to vitamin A within the body). Carrots are a great snack food.

Cauliflower

Known for its anti-inflammatory properties, high levels of anti-oxidants and as a great detoxification food, cauliflower also contains vitamins B1, B2, B3, B5, B6, B9, C and K. It contains omega-3 fatty acids and serves as a good source of proteins, phosphorus, manganese and potassium.

Celery

Celery is a great weight-loss food known for its diuretic quality. It also helps boost immunity because of its high vitamin C content. A great food to snack on to keep the common cold at bay. Celery is very low in cholesterol. It is also a good source of riboflavin, vitamins A, B6, C and K, calcium, magnesium and phosphorus, and a very good source of dietary fibre, folate, potassium and manganese.

Corn (Sweet Corn) Kernels

Corn (sweet corn) kernels are packed with nutrients including vitamin A, B and C, as well as fibre. Iron also contains an abundance of carbohydrates. Make sure the husks appear green and fresh. A great food to use as a topping for pizza instead of cheese.

Cucumber

Cucumbers are rich in vitamins A, B1, B6, C and D, folate, calcium, magnesium and potassium. Being largely made up of water, they rehydrate the body and replenish vitamins. The skin contains high levels of vitamin C.

Cucumbers are 95 per cent water, so help keep the body hydrated while aiding the elimination of toxins. Cucumbers have most of the vitamins the body needs. Don't forget to leave the skin on because cucumber also contains a generous amount of vitamin C.

Garlic

Garlic was traditionally used to ward off illnesses. Today, it is still thought of as a cure for the common cold, infections, indigestion… and the list goes on. As a natural curative, garlic enjoys a lot of attention in many parts of the world. It's also extremely popular because it offers an easy way to add flavour to many dishes. Garlic is intrinsic to the cuisine of many food cultures. The plant has a high anti-oxidant value.

Kale

Kale is a nutritional powerhouse that is beneficial to the body in so many ways. It is high in vitamins A, B6, C, K, and calcium, potassium, copper and manganese. High in anti-oxidants, kale helps strengthen the immune system. The fibre in kale lowers cholesterol and is a good source of dietary fibre.

Mushrooms, Fresh and Dried

Mushrooms are packed with selenium, an anti-oxidant and trace element that promotes healing and, when combined with vitamin E, protects the body from harmful free radicals. Mushrooms contain folate, zinc, potassium, copper, magnesium and vitamin B6. Much of the mushroom's flavour lies just below the skin. Never wash mushrooms, since this fungi absorbs water. Instead always wipe them with a damp cloth.

Onions

Rich in vitamins B6 and C, and an excellent source of chromium and sulphuric compounds, onions lower insulin levels and improve tolerance for glucose. They help maintain healthy bones, which is great for anyone at risk of osteoporosis. Onions are known to reduce inflammation and the high vitamin C and flavonoid content work together to kill bacteria.

   Store onions at room temperature, in a dark space that is well ventilated. Do not store them with potatoes because they pick up their moisture and lead to faster decay. Store cut onions in a sealed container or bag, eat within 2 days or they will lose their nutritional value quickly due to oxidation.

Rocket (Arugula)

Rocket is rich in vitamins A and C. Vitamin A provides beta-carotene, which help to protect cells from damage and create anti-oxidants in the body. Rocket is also high in fibre, calcium, folate, and phytonutrients that are excellent for liver health. The vitamin C content provides powerful and natural anti-oxidants to help protect the body from illness and disease.

Salad Leaves

Eating dark leafy salad greens can help detoxify and refuel your body with powerful nutrients. All green leaves are beneficial, the darker ones more so. Salad leaves contain anti-oxidants, vitamins C and E, and folic acid.

Shallots

Eating shallots regularly can contribute to lowering cholesterol levels, improving blood circulation and reducing the risk of cardiovascular disease. These alliums are a rich source of vitamins A, B and E. They contain iron, which is required for proper functioning of the red blood cells. Eating them regularly promotes a healthy digestive system.

Spinach (English)

Rich in a vitamins A, K and folate, a serving of **Raw** spinach provides more than the daily requirement for vitamin K, which is important for proper blood clotting. Folate is important for women in preparing for pregnancy.

Spring Onions (Scallions)

Rich in vitamins A, B1, B12, C and K. The sulphur compounds in spring onions can help control blood pressure levels and reduce cholesterol. The chromium content improves glucose tolerance and helps regulate blood sugar levels. Because of their high vitamin content, spring onions help to protect against colds and flu and will help boost the immune system.

Squash

Squash is a good source of protein, vitamins A, B6, C and K, and a very good source of dietary fibre, magnesium, potassium and manganese.

Sugarsnap Peas

Rich in vitamin K, sugarsnap peas help the bones retain calcium. They also contain vitamin B6 and C, and overall are good for heart health. They provide anti-oxidants that can help to protect against the growth of cancer cells.

Sweet Potatoes

A great source of vitamins A and C as well as potassium and iron, sweet potatoes are a great food to eat when you want something sweet.

Tomatoes Including Sun-Dried Tomatoes
Tomatoes are rich in the anti-oxidant known as lyocpene. There are so many varieties of tomatoes available all year round. At their best they are sweet, juicy and flavourful, a powerhouse of dietary fibre and vitamins.

Zucchini (Courgettes)
Zucchini aids digestion; it is high in dietary fibre, prevents constipation and helps maintains blood. It contains vitamins A and C, as well as folate. A serving of zucchini contains 10 per cent of the recommended daily allowance of magnesium and folate, which helps to reduce the risk of heart attack and stroke. Zucchini is high in manganese, a trace mineral and essential nutrient.

Fresh and Dried Fruit

Apples
This staple and inexpensive food is a good source of dietary fibre and vitamin C. It has a low glycaemic value, providing sustained energy for the body. Apples are high in potassium, essential minerals, and vitamin B.

Apricots
Apricots contain dietary fibre and potassium, and are a very good source of vitamins A and C. They are high in anti-oxidants and beta-carotene and support digestive health.

Bananas
Bananas are a good snack food and a great dessert replacement, because of their sweetness. Very low in saturated fat, cholesterol and sodium and a good source of dietary fibre, vitamin C, potassium and manganese, and a rich source of vitamin B6, potassium protects against cardiovascular disease. Bananas are soothing for the digestive system and may help you to feel calm.

Blueberries
Blueberries are considered a superfood and readily available all year around. The dark blue colour is the clue to the high levels of manganese, fibre and vitamin C.

Coconut (Young)
Young or green coconuts provide calcium, iron, zinc, potassium, phosphorous, magnesium and vitamins B1, B2, B3, B5, B6, folate and vitamin C. People in the tropics have relied on coconuts

to treat diabetes, chronic fatigue, Crohn's disease, irritable bowel syndrome (IBS) and digestive disorders. Coconuts are thought to boost energy levels, support the immune function and to rejuvenate the body.

Coconut: Desiccated (Dry, Unsweetened, Shredded)

This sweet and dried product provides minerals that help to keep connective tissues strong. The copper in the desiccated coconut is a superfood supporting the brain function.

Cranberries (Dried)

Another superfood, high in anti-oxidants which help flush out toxins from the body. Cranberries are thought to be anti-ageing. Cranberry juice can help prevent urinary tract infections. These tart fruits help nourish the body. They're rich in carbohydrates, proteins, minerals, calcium, phosphorus, iron, magnesium and zinc.

Dates (Fresh and Dried)

Dates are a useful and popular Raw food, often used as a natural sweetener. They are a great source of vitamins and minerals, calcium, iron, phosphorus, sodium, potassium, magnesium and zinc. They also contain folate, vitamins A, K, riboflavin, thiamin and niacin.

Grapes

Eat grapes for a boost of vitamin C, a powerful anti-oxidant that helps counteract the body of free radicals. Grapes contain vitamin B1, flavonoids, potassium and manganese. They are known to boost immunity as well as energy. Grapes keep the nervous system functioning properly.

Goji Berries

Used in Chinese medicine for more than 6000 years, goji berries are nutritional gold. They are mostly sold dried. Eat them to boost your immune system, improve brain function, reduce the risk of heart disease and cancer. They provide a great source of vitamins A and C, as well as iron and fibre.

Kiwi Fruits

Rich in vitamins and minerals, vitamin C, potassium and fibre, kiwis, also known as Chinese gooseberries, contain lutein, which is an incredible anti-oxidant known to attack free radicals, and helping to prevent disease. The skin is edible, highly nutritious and full of fibre. A kiwi fruit contains about as much potassium as a banana. Potassium helps to regulate bodily fluids, electrolytes and acidity.

Lemons

This alkalising food has a high vitamin C content, as well as being rich in potassium, anti-oxidants, and folate. Together they help to strengthen the immune system. Lemons are great for cleansing the internal body and have powerful anti-bacterial properties.

Limes

Limes are high in vitamin C and calcium. One medium lime contains about 22 mg of calcium, which is a significant quantity of the daily dietary requirement. Limes are a good source of phytonutrients and other nutrients and trace minerals. The beautiful citrus flavour is often used in **Raw** recipes.

Mandarins

Mandarins are full of vitamin C and anti-oxidants, which help mop up free radicals in the body. They are a great source of dietary fibre, helping you to feel fuller for longer. A great weight-loss food.

Mangoes

Mangos are a rich source of vitamin A (100 g/3½ oz of the fruit provides 25 per cent of the day's vitamin A, which is essential for healthy vision, as well as vitamins B6, C and E. Mangos are also high in carotene and potassium, which help control blood pressure.

Oranges

Renowned for the vitamin C content, oranges also contain flavonoids, B-complex vitamins and are rich in dietary fibre, which helps to protect the colon. Eating oranges will help prevent anaemia.

Peaches

Like other fruits, peaches are full of sweet flavour. They contain no fat and are packed with nutritional goodness. Their vitamin A content helps provide healthy vision, the vitamin C content promotes tissue building, and vitamin K assists blood clotting. Additionally, peaches contain the minerals magnesium, phosphorous, zinc, copper, manganese, iron and calcium.

Pineapple

Sweet and flavourful pineapples are loaded with vitamins and minerals. They are high in fibre and low in fat and cholesterol. The compound bromelain is present in pineapple, which helps ease inflammation. Pineapples are abundant in dietary fibre too.

Raisins

Raisins have many health benefits but are also high in sugar so eat them in moderation. They contain no fat and are very high in dietary fibre. They contain essential B vitamins as well as vitamin C and K.

Raspberries (Frozen)

When raspberries are harvested and snap frozen all their nutrients are locked in. Fresh raspberries can lose their potent nutrients within 10 days of harvesting. Frozen berries are recognised as being nutritionally equal to Raw and in some cases even more nutritious. Frozen raspberries are very high in fibre and anti-oxidants, contain several B vitamins, vitamin C and K and the minerals calcium, magnesium, phosphorus and potassium.

Strawberries

This sweet berry is a fleeting summer favourite best picked and enjoyed straightaway. Strawberries are an excellent source of vitamins C and K, dietary fibre and flavonoids. Buy or grow organic strawberries to limit your contact with the harmful pesticides this crop is sprayed with.

Watermelon

Watermelon is made up predominantly of water but for all that it is still considered a nutrient-dense food with high amounts of vitamins, minerals, and anti-oxidants. Consumption of watermelon has been known to lower the risk of asthma and high blood pressure.

Fresh and Dried Herbs, Spices and Seasonings

Basil

Basil is often referred to as the king of herbs. It is high in flavonoids and the leaves contain essential oils, which have anti-inflammatory and anti-bacterial properties. Basil is also high in iron, vitamin K and essential minerals, great for heart health.

Cayenne Pepper

Cayenne pepper is commonly used in cleansing and detoxing programmes. It is lovely sprinkled into a lemon drink. This spice helps to stimulate circulation and improve digestion by increasing stomach acids and enzyme secretion. It is known to normalise blood pressure and cholesterol levels.

Cinnamon

This spice has been found to help keep blood sugar levels balanced. It helps stimulate digestion and appetite, relieves indigestion, excess wind and nausea, and is beneficial for alleviating diarrhoea and help an upset stomach.

Cardamom

Cardamom is rich and warming. It's the perfect spice to add to milk-type drinks.

Chilli powder and chilli flakes

Use chilli powder and chilli flakes to add heat to your meals.

Cloves

Cloves help soothe an upset stomach and help aid digestion. They have an anti-microbial action, which helps rid the digestive tract of unwanted bacteria.

Coriander and Cilantro (Fresh and Dried)

Coriander acts as a natural antibiotic. It is usually associated with Eastern dishes and adds a large flavour punch to any recipe.

Cumin

Cumin is rich in iron and vitamin C. It supports the immune function and helps the liver detoxify.

Curry powder

Like chilli powder, curry adds heat and spice.

Garlic and garlic powder

The health benefits of garlic are extensive. This herb is used the world over as a healing herb and to add flavour to food.

Ginger, root and powder

Ginger root is pungent, adding intense flavour to foods. It has healing qualities too. Add to meals or drink as an infusion. The powder is less intense.

Mint

Mint contains powerful anti-oxidants. It adds a refreshing taste to salads and to tea. A very useful herb to grow and available in plenty of species.

Oregano

Oregano is rich in vitamin K and helps the body fight infection. It has anti-inflammatory properties too.

Paprika

A little paprika goes a long way. This spice with its intense red colour can be used to add heat to food and decoration to plates.

Parsley

Parsley is high in anti-oxidants and rich in vitamins A, C and K, as well as the minerals folic acid, calcium, iron and potassium. The high content of vitamin K plays a role in maintaining strong bones.

Pepper

Eating black pepper is known to increase your mineral and phytonutrient intake and might reduce your risk of disease.

Rosemary

Rosemary is traditionally thought to help boost memory and concentration as well as relieve stress. It is stimulating and warming and is thought to help with the circulation. Rosemary contains high levels of anti-oxidants and has anti-microbial properties.

Salt: Himalayan Pink Salt or Celtic Sea Salt

Pink in colour Himalayan salt is considered healthier than common table salt because it does not contain any additives or chemicals, and is a naturally occurring substance.

Star Anise

This spice has a licorice-like flavour. The smell is divine and it too is a healing herb.

Thyme

Thyme has strong anti-bacterial and anti-microbial action.

Turmeric Root and Powder

Turmeric is a spice with amazing anti-oxidant properties, protecting the body from damage inflicted by free radicals. It also supports the liver function and the immune system.

Vanilla Pod (Bean) and Vanilla Extract

Vanilla contains high levels of antioxidants, can help alleviate anxiety, and is known to stimulate sexual desire.

Nuts

Almonds
Almonds contain a large quantity of protein and are an excellent source of vitamins B and E, magnesium and fibre, copper, calcium, potassium, phosphorus and iron.

They help to lower the rise in blood sugar and insulin that occurs naturally in the body after eating. They help provide good brain function and eating them regularly may help to reduce the risk of Alzheimer's disease. Almonds nourish the nervous system. They are the only nut and one of only a few proteins that are alkaline-forming.

Brazil Nuts
Brazil nuts, like all nuts, have a high calorific content and should be eaten in moderation. These nuts are an excellent source of mono-unsaturated fatty acids that help to lower LDL (low-density lipoprotein) or 'bad cholesterol' and increases HDL (high-density lipoprotein) or 'good cholesterol' in the blood. Brazil nuts contain exceptionally high levels of selenium, which helps prevent coronary artery disease, liver cirrhosis and cancers.

Cashews
Sweet and crunchy delicious cashew nuts are packed with energy, anti-oxidants, minerals, vitamins and soluble dietary fibre. Cashew butter is a fabulous alternative to standard butter. Why not give it a try?

Hazelnuts
Eating hazelnuts can reduce the risk of cardiovascular disease possibly on account of the high mono-unsaturated fat content. Hazelnuts are rich in vitamin E and minerals such as copper and magnesium, all of which help reduce blood pressure and inflammation.

LSA (Linseeds, Sunflower Seeds and Almonds)
LSA help to cleanse and detoxify the liver. The liver is the cleanser and filter of the bloodstream, it regulates fat metabolism and makes HDL cholesterol (good cholesterol), which carries the LDL (bad cholesterol) back to the liver for elimination. One to two tablespoons of LSA per day added to breakfast cereal, yogurt or smoothies will increase that food's nutrient value significantly. Alternatively, sprinkle LSA on salads and fruit.

Macadamia Nuts
Loaded with good fats, when eaten in balance macadamias provide a unique source of key nutrients and are good for your heart health.

Pecans
Pecan nuts are a very rich source of several important B-complex vitamins. Eating pecans regularly helps to decrease cholesterol. Pecans have a sweet and buttery flavour.

Pine Nuts
Pine nuts are the smallest of nuts with a sweet, subtle flavour. They are rich in healthy fats and are full of anti-oxidants.

Pistachio Nuts
Pistachios pack a powerful nutritional punch, containing protein and fibre as well as a beneficial vitamins and minerals.

Walnuts
Walnuts have an acquired taste that is often bitter. They offer a rich source of heart-healthy mono-unsaturated fats and an excellent source of omega-3 fatty acids. Add to salad, fruit or desserts.

Seeds

Chia
Chia is high in protein, omega-3 fatty acids and fibre. These seeds also contains the essential minerals phosphorous, manganese, calcium, potassium and sodium.

Flax (Linseeds)
Flax (linseeds) are the richest source of omega-3 essential fatty acids. Linseeds improve the quality of hair, nails and skin.

Hemp
Hemp seeds are an incredible vegan source of biologically available and easily digested protein. For those who are allergic to soy, hemp seeds are a great vegan alternative. They are rich in vitamin E and minerals including zinc, calcium, phosphorous, magnesium and iron and a anti-inflammatory food source.

Pumpkin
High in zinc and important for prostate health, pumpkin seeds are also rich in magnesium, omega-3 fats and anti-oxidants.

Sunflower
Sunflower seeds are packed with healthy minerals including selenium, and promote good bone health.

Sesame
A good source of protein and packed with essential vitamins and minerals that help prevent disease and support overall health. Especially good for for those seeking plant-based protein.

Grains and Legumes

Amaranth
Amaranth boosts the immune function. It is rich in vitamins A, B6, C and K.

Brown Rice
Brown rice is less refined than white rice and is much easier to digest. It contains a host of minerals and trace elements. It is great for releasing energy slowly.

Buckwheat
Buckwheat offers the best source of high quality, easily digestible proteins. Try buckwheat soaked with almond milk and served with berries for a nourishing, energizing and tasty food in place of porridge; it will change your body and energy.

Chickpeas
Chickpeas are a rich source of protein, manganese, iron, and fibre. They have a lovely nutty flavour.

Freekeh
Freekeh is an ancient green cracked wheat grain that is low in carbohydrate, has a low GI and low fat, while high in fibre, protein, calcium, iron and zinc. Freekeh does contain gluten, however, it is highly beneficial and 100 per cent natural.

Kamut
Kamut is a versatile grain with a nutty flavour. It provides protein, fibre and minerals.

Kefir

Kefir grains are a combination of lactic acid bacteria and resemble cauliflower. Kefir contains protein, vitamins A, B1, B2, B6, D and K, as well as folic acid, calcium, iron and iodine. Kefir is made into dairy-free yogurt, which boosts the health of the digestive system and eating it helps reduce sugar cravings. People with lactose intolerance are able to tolerate kefir.

Lentils

Available in different varieties, lentils are an inexpensive food that are rich in protein. They will keep you feeling full for a long time.

Millet

Millet is a grain used in bread-making.

Quinoa

Pronounced 'keen-wah', this superfood is gluten free, nutritious and high in protein. It adds body and texture to any **Raw** food recipe, and has a lovely nutty flavour. Quinoa grains are the grain-like sprouts of a plant similar to Swiss chard and spinach. Rinse the quinoa seeds thoroughly before using them.

Spelt

This is the oldest grain used for bread-making. Spelt grains are easier on the stomach since the quantity of gluten it contains is less than modern wheat.

Supplements

Vegetarians and **Raw** foodies may be low in vitamin B12, so if you follow this lifestyle take a vitamin everyday that includes B12. I believe that taking supplements is vital in today's world. Yet often people take supplements hoping to improve their health, but they don't get the results they want because in reality they need to change and improve their diet.

Are you eating certified organic food?

Are you drinking filtered water?

Are you exposed to toxins in your environment?

Are you confident that you are getting the required amount of magnesium daily in your daily nutrition regime?

The truth is simple, there is no guarantee that the fruits and vegetables you choose to eat have been grown in mineral-rich soil, or that they contain maximum nutrients to provide you with the vitamins and trace elements your body needs to survive and live without disease.

Greens Powder

Add greens powder to smoothies to increase nutrients and taste or have it on its own diluted in water. Most greens powders include a blend of alkalising grasses, such as barley grass, wheat grass, alfalfa leaf, kale powder and broccoli and are sweetened with apple powder and celery-raspberry powder. This food supplement is great to take if you are worried about eating enough protein in your **Raw** food diet.

Lecithin Granules

Lecithin granules are used medically to manage cholesterol and weight loss, and provide many health benefits such as age-related memory loss, heart health and weight loss. This supplement boosts brain development. Lecithin granules are made from **Raw**, natural liquid lecithin combined with soy flour and other compatible food substances to make a nutrient-rich food supplement. These granules can be sprinkled on cereal and salads, or added to protein drinks and juices.

As a bread and dough enhancer lecithin improves the moisture tolerance and uniform suspension of ingredients. It stabilizes fats and oils, reducing rancidity and prolongs freshness.

Maca Powder

Maca is a root vegetable and medicinal herb. For the purposes of a **Raw** food lifestyle it is supplied as a nutritional superfood supplement in powder form that acts as a tonic on the body. It has beneficial qualities, modulating hormones and promoting energy. Maca powder is made from the Peruvian root and is a dense superfood that contains high amounts of minerals, vitamins, enzymes and essential amino acids. It is rich in B vitamin, a vegetarian source of B12 and offers an energy boost.

Nutritional (Savoury) Yeast

This deactivated yeast is sold in flakes or as powder. It provides B vitamins.

Probiotics

Empty the powder from the capsule and incorporate it into your recipe. Probiotics are friendly bacteria that we need to consume for good health and vitality and improve the balance of flora in the gut. Probiotics improve digestion, help relieve the symptoms of irritable bowel syndrome (IBS), repair the gut lining; increasing resistance to infections and regulating immune function.

Spirulina

Spirulina is a food supplement derived from a plant. It contains vitamins, minerals and eight amino acids as well as anti-oxidants. It's great to add to smoothies.

Sprouting Grains and Legumes

Sprouting is the method of germinating grains or legumes that will be eaten Raw. They are a prominent ingredient in the Raw food way of life. The most common food sprouts include pulses, legumes, and the pea family including, alfalfa, clover, fenugreek, lentil, pea, chickpea, mung bean, and soya beansprouts. Cereals including oats, rice, barley, kamut, quinoa, amaranth and buckwheat can also be sprouted. All viable seeds can be sprouted, but some sprouts should not be eaten Raw. Avoid any that have turned brown.

Add two-thirds of a cup of grain or legume to your seed sprouter or to a glass bowl. Cover with filtered water and leave for 6 hours or overnight. Rinse thoroughly to remove the saponin (chemical compounds) from the grain or legume, then transfer to a clean seed sprouter or glass bowl. Cover again with cool filtered water (the temperature should be no warmer than 21°C (70°F) and leave to stand for 30 minutes. Drain and rinse again.

Transfer the grain or legume to a large tray or plate, cover and set aside in a darker area at room temperature. Rinse and drain the grain or legume every 8–12 hours over the next 2 days.

Transfer the grains or legumes to a glass bowl, cover with cool filtered water and set aside for 30 minutes. Drain, transfer to a plate and leave to dry.

Cover and return the grain or legume to a dark space to continue the sprouting process. Eventually the grain or legume will sprout into a plateful of spiral-shaped roots that are at least ¼ in (0.5 cm) long. Once sprouted, let the quinoa sprouts dry out for up to 12 hours, since excess moisture damages the crop.

Store in a sealed mason jar or glass container and place in the refrigerator.

Quinoa stays fresh for up to two weeks after sprouting. I do this process with chickpeas; soak overnight, drain, rinse and repeat. You can use the chickpeas straightaway for dips, hummus or to sprinkle in salads, or again dry out and store in glass jars.

A Note About Bread

Since becoming a **Raw** foodie and vegetarian, I found it hard to give up bread, though it always made me feel bloated and gain weight. I now enjoy gluten-free crisp breads, and have learned how to make and ferment sourdough.

Grinding Flour

You can make your own flours by grinding the grains in the bowl of a food processor until a fine flour is formed. Store grain flour in the refrigerator or freezer to stop it from going rancid. The following nuts and grains can be ground into nutritious, gluten-free flour and are great for the Sourdough recipe. I recommend almonds, quinoa, spelt and chickpeas.

Oils

Almond Oil

Widely used in beauty products, almond oil, contains mono-unsaturated omega-9 fatty acid, which keeps skin supple and hair in good order. Drizzle almond oil on salads to benefit from this vitamin-rich ingredient.

Coconut Oil

Raw, cold-pressed coconut oil adds authentic tropical flavour to Asian dishes. It is a heart-healthy oil for culinary purposes as long as you buy the unrefined version. Avoid coconut oil if you have heart disease, kidney disease or if you are following a low potassium diet.

Flaxseed Oil

Flaxseed, or linseed, oil is made from crushing the seeds of the flax plant. While not widely used as cooking oil, it retains phytoestrogens, which are considered to have anti-oxidant and cancer-preventing properties. It contains the highest level of the alpha-linoleic acid of all the vegetable oils, which may be beneficial for preventing heart disease and maintaining a healthy heart.

Hemp Seed Oil

Derived from the seeds of the Asian hemp plant, hemp seed oil is of high nutritional value, containing beneficial proportions of both omega-6 and omega-3 essential fatty acids, while remaining low in saturated fats. Its excellent as a **Raw** food oil.

Olive Oil

The olive is a fruit and its oil is characterized by a very high oleic acid (a mono-unsaturated oil) content and is widely recognised as being protective against heart disease. Olive oil is sold in varying degrees of refinement, with extra virgin olive oil being the first pressing of the fruit. It is highly nutritious.

Sweeteners

Agave Nectar

The agave plant is an American desert plant. Agave nectar is sweet, with a lower glycaemic value than sugar. It also contains inulin, which may assist with inflammation and increase the absorption of nutrients. Be aware of using agave, as it is very high in fructose and should only be used occasionally. If you consume too much high fructose sugar, your body can end up craving more sugar. The best way to eliminate sugar cravings is to eliminate sugar.

Dates

Dates have been used to add taste, sweetness and a touch of exotic flavour to food since medieval times. Dates are high in calories, but also in potassium, and contain some vitamin B6, niacin, iron and magnesium.

Maple Syrup

Maple syrup is made from the sap of the maple tree, which has been reduced by boiling. It is then crystallized into a sticky sugar. True maple syrup consists partly of dextrose and partly of fructose. This product provides a more gradual release of energy than sugar, which may help stabilise mood and appetite.

Honey, Raw and Manuka

Honey is the earliest known sweetener, produced by bees, after being collected as nectar from flowers. Its main component is fructose, but its rich flavour is also derived from the flowers on which the bees feed. Manuka honey is from New Zealand, and has renowned antibacterial properties.

Miscellaneous

Almond Extract

Unlike almond nuts, almond extract does not contain oils. It contains B vitamins and potassium and adds a pleasant flavour to food.

Apple Cider Vinegar

Apple cider vinegar is one of the large family of vinegars historically used in food preparation and is created by fermenting the natural crushed fruit syrup.

Balsamic Vinegar

Balsamic vinegar is thick black vinegar available in various grades and with different price points. It may help lower and stabilise blood pressure. It is low in fats and calories so can be used more often than oils to add flavour to **Raw** foods.

Cacao Powder and Nibs (Organic Raw)

Cacao beans are a rich source of anti-oxidants. However, when they are turned into cocoa, they are roasted and in the process the beans lose some of the nutrients.

Both cacao and cocoa are high in anti-oxidants. Each contain theobromine, which helps to dilate blood vessels encouraging oxygen to flow to all parts of the body. Theobromine has been proven to reduce symptoms of asthma and lower blood pressure. Cacao is rich in magnesium, an element that plays a big role in bone health, heart health and for more than 280 biochemical reactions in your body.

Nibs are a **Raw** derivative of organic chocolate, similar to chocolate chips.

Please note: Don't consume more than 1¼ oz (40 g) (or four to six heaped teaspoons) of **Raw** cacao a day.

Coconut Water

This is the water from a young green coconut. It's a nutritional goldmine, full of natural electrolytes, and is cholesterol free. It is low in fat and carbs. It contains zinc, selenium, iodine, sulphur, manganese, ascorbic acid, and B-group vitamins.

Coconut water promotes smoother and more youthful skin, can improve blood circulation, is great for a healthy digestive system and urinary health.

Coconut Milk

Coconut milk is the liquid that comes from the grated (shredded) meat of a brown coconut whereas coconut water is the watery liquid that usually comes from the immature green coconut.

Filtered Water

I recommended filtered drinking water over purified water; numerous studies have shown that mineral-rich drinking water is the healthiest.

Nama Shoya

Nama shoyu is raw, unpasteurized soy sauce.

Nori

Nori can be eaten on its own or in salads,wrapped around raw veggies or quinoa and brown rice. Eat in moderate amounts. It is rich in iron.

Olives, Black and Kalamata

The fat in black olives is heart-healthy; these fats may lower LDL or 'bad' cholesterol levels and increase HDL or 'good' cholesterol levels.

Onion Powder

Onion powder is made from dehydrated onions, giving it a concentrated flavor that pairs well with many foods.

Tahini

Tahini is a paste made from ground sesame seeds, and is a source of healthy fatty acids.

Tamari

Soy sauce and tamari are made from fermented soy beans. It is a good source of vitamin B3, protein, manganese, and tryptophan.

Equipment

Sharp Knife
Sharp knives are essential for preparing vegetables. Choose a good quality brand.

Fine Mesh Strainer
Use when making nut milks and cheeses.

Cutting Board
Keep a separate board for cutting members of the onion family so that the potent smell of onions doesn't contaminate other ingredients.

Measuring Cups/Weigh Scales
Use for accurate weighing and measuring.

Blender or Food Processor
I use a Vitamix blender with thermo mix for efficiency. A standard blender may be used for processing but it is not optimal. A blender is used to emulsify foods. A processor is used to mix ingredients and prepare crusts, flours, pesto, dips or anything that will retain some texture. The base of all my food preparation is done with a processor, with a blender for the soups and smoothies. A Vitamix can grind dry ingredients, but doesn't work as well for smaller quantities. You can also use mini processors or even a coffee grinder, though don't use the same one that is used by the family for grinding coffee, since the taste will carry to the food you are preparing.

Dehydrator
If you are beginning your Raw food journey you like to source an inexpensive dehydrator to see how you get on. I used an oven at the beginning of my journey to make the cripbreads. However, since owning a dehydrator I value the benefits of this method, which include a greater control of products that might dry out faster in a conventional oven than they would with the dehydrator, thereby losing essential nutrients.

A dehydrator is used to 'bake' or dehydrate food ready for eating. Use it to make crisp breads and it will soon become a staple item of your cookware. Use the dehydrator in conjunction with Teflex sheets, which are silicone-coated sheets, that stop the food falling through the trays in the dehydrator. If you don't have a dehydrator you can cheat and use the electric oven set on its lowest setting. Dehydrators are inexpensive and easy to use.

Sterilizing Glass Storage Containers

Glass is the best vessel in which to store juices, smoothies, dips and sauces. Sterilize the jars before using them to help prevent contamination. Wash the glass in hot soapy water. Rinse well. Place the jars and lids in a deep saucepan. Cover with cold water. Bring the water to the boil. Reduce the heat to medium and boil gently for 10 minutes.

Preheat the oven 115°C/240°F. Line a baking tray with a clean kitchen towel. Using metal tongs, remove the jars and lids from the boiling water and place upside down on the tray. Place in the oven for 15 minutes.

Spiral slicer

These are becoming very popular as a means of cutting vegetables into noodle shapes. You don't have to go without 'pasta' if you have one of these handy devices. Use to make curly 'noodles' from zucchini or squash. This gadget helps to make **Raw** food look amazing.

Chapter One

1 NUTS

Nuts are packed with nutritional value, and an essential part of any **Raw** foodie's diet. Almonds, in particular, are a great source of protein, fibre, vitamin E, omegas-3 and 6 fatty acids, calcium, magnesium and zinc. However, consuming too many **Raw** nuts that still have their skin on makes it difficult for your digestive system to break them down. Almonds also have an enzyme-inhibiting substance in their brown coating, making them difficult to digest. Soaking, sprouting or activating the nuts removes this inhibitor.

Cashew Nut Milk

The great thing about making cashew nut milk is that you don't need to strain it. It tastes delicious on its own with a Raw **chocolate cookie or blended into a healthy smoothie.**

1 cup (4 oz/115 g) cashew nuts, soaked for 2 hours
3 cups (24 fl oz/750 ml) filtered water
½ vanilla bean (pod)
1 tablespoon honey or 1 fresh date
¼ teaspoon Himalayan pink salt or Celtic sea salt

Blend all the ingredients in the bowl of a food processor or blender until smooth, then strain through muslin or a nut bag. Store in a glass container in the refrigerator for up to 2 days.

Activating Nuts
Rinse the nuts, soak overnight in filtered water, drain but retain the liquid, then rub off the skins. Alternatively, tip the almonds into a glass or ceramic bowl, pour over boiling filtered water and set aside for 10 minutes. Drain, cool and squeeze the skin so that it will easily pop off.

NOTE: Be aware of how many nuts you consume. Nuts are high in fat. Keep them for a once-a-week treat.

Coconut Milk

If you like the flavour of coconut, then this is the milk to try.

½ cup (1½ oz/45 g) desiccated (dry, unsweetened, shredded) coconut
1 pint (600 ml) filtered water
1 fresh date
Seeds from ½ vanilla bean (pod)
¼ teaspoon Himalayan pink salt or Celtic sea salt

Blend all the ingredients in the bowl of a food processor or blender until smooth, then strain through muslin or a nut bag. Store in a glass container in the refrigerator for up to 2 days.

Almond Milk

For smooth almond milk I like to soak the almonds first in hot water for 10 minutes, and then remove the skins by rubbing the nuts in a clean kitchen cloth. Blend and make the almond milk. This saves the process of straining the almond milk through the nut bag.

1 cup (4 oz/115 g) almonds
1 tablespoon coconut oil (optional)
1 teaspoon lecithin granules
1 fresh date
1 teaspoon vanilla extract
¼ teaspoon Himalayan pink salt or Celtic sea salt

Blend all the ingredients in the bowl of a food processor or blender until smooth, then strain through muslin or a nut bag. Store in a glass container in the refrigerator for up to 2 days.

Brazil Nut Milk

Brazil nuts are a source of good fats, and great to use for a cream substitute. Brazil nut milk is highly nutritious and a good replacement for those who can't go without their dairy products.

4 cups (1¾ pints/1 litre) filtered water
1 cup (4 oz/115 g) Brazil nuts, soaked in water for 5 hours, rinsed and drained
2 dates, pits removed
1 tablespoon coconut oil, or ½ cup (1½ oz/45 g) desiccated (dry, unsweetened, shredded) coconut
¼ teaspoon Himalayan pink salt or Celtic sea salt
1 teaspoon vanilla extract

Place the water, nuts, dates, coconut, salt and vanilla in a high speed blender and process until smooth and creamy. Pour the nut milk into a large bowl through a strainer lined with muslin or a nut bag. Discard the pulp or dehydrate it ready to add to breakfast.

This milk will keep in the refrigerator for 2–3 days. Shake the milk before you drink it as it will separate.

Almond Butter

A great dairy butter substitute, use this nut butter as a spread on crisp breads, sourdoughs, or open sandwiches.

1 cup (4 oz/115 g) activated almonds (see recipe)
½ cup (4 fl oz/125 ml) flaxseed oil
¼ teaspoon Himalayan pink salt or Celtic sea salt

Blend all the ingredients together in the bowl of a blender or food processor until smooth. Use as a spread or butter.

Cashew Chia Butter

A great spread for toast, sandwiches or pancakes.

1 cup (4 oz/115 g) cashew nuts
1 teaspoon honey
¼ teaspoon Himalayan pink salt or Celtic sea salt

Blend all the ingredients together in the bowl of a blender or food processor until smooth.

Hazelnut Butter

Use as a spread on pancakes, or crisp breads.

1 cup (4 oz/115 g) hazelnuts
1 teaspoon olive oil

Blend all the ingredients together in the bowl of a blender or food processor until smooth.

Chapter Two

2 BREADS

Raw Tortilla Wraps

The flavour of the spices and fresh salad with the wrap texture is divine. Eating Raw is about creating textures, that you'll become more aware of on your Raw food journey.

Makes 5

1½ cups (5 oz/150 g) yellow squash
⅓ cup (1½ oz/45 g) chia seeds
⅓ cup (1½ oz/45 g) LSA meal (mixed ground linseeds, sunflower seeds and almonds)
1 tomato
2 tablespoons olive oil
1 garlic clove
1 teaspoon chilli powder
½ teaspoon cumin powder
Himalayan pink salt or Celtic sea salt

Place all the ingredients in the bowl of a blender or food processor. Turn the speed to low then quickly increase it to high speed. Stop frequently to scrape down the ingredients. Blend until smooth.

Spread the batter into rounds as thin or as thick as you like on Teflex sheets or baking paper and then place on the dehydrator trays covered with non-stick baking paper.

Dry the wraps at 65°C/150°F for 2 hours, then flip them over and continue drying for another 2 hours. Dry until the wrap is still moist and easy to lift up. Store in the refrigerator for up to several weeks.

Kim's Kale Crisp Bread

This is one of my favourite and most popular recipes because is it is crispy, salty and tasty.
Spread with mashed avocado, then top with Raw tomato and basil leaves.

Makes 1 large tray (24 squares)

1 cup (2¼ oz/65 g) kale
½ cup (½ oz/15 g) English spinach
4 fresh basil leaves
2 cups (8 oz/225 g) LSA meal (mixed ground linseeds, sunflower seeds and almonds)
⅓ cup (1½ oz/45 g) pumpkin seeds
⅓ cup (1¾ oz/50 g) sunflower seeds
¼ teaspoon chilli flakes
1 teaspoon dried oregano
1 teaspoon cumin
1 tablespoon olive oil, plus extra for greasing
½ teaspoon Himalayan pink salt or Celtic sea salt
Hummus, to serve
Salad, to serve

Preheat the oven to 150°C/300°F, and line or grease a baking sheet.

Process the kale and spinach in the bowl of a food processor or blender then tip into a large bowl.

Process the remaining ingredients until a dough forms. Add to the greens and mix together. Tip out
onto the lined baking paper, place a sheet of baking paper on top, then roll over with a rolling pin
until smooth and ¼ in (0.5 cm) thick.

Bake for 20 minutes at 75°C/170°F, or dehydrate until crispy, about 1 hour.

Spiced Kale and Pumpkin Seed Crackers

Looking for something with a little bite and spice to it? This recipe is great for serving as a starter with dips. I like to serve these crackers with lettuce, spinach, diced tomato, chopped coriander and Spanish onion for a snack or easy dinner.

Serves 6–8

2 cups (10 oz/280 g) pumpkin seeds
1 cup (2¼ oz/65 g) kale or spinach, shredded
1 teaspoon lime or lemon juice
1 tablespoon ginger
1 teaspoon ground coriander
1 teaspoon garlic powder
1 teaspoon onion powder
⅛ teaspoon chilli flakes
2 tablespoons gluten-free tamari soy sauce
½ teaspoon Himalayan pink salt or Celtic sea salt
¼ cup (1¼ oz/40 g) flax meal or LSA meal (mixed ground linseeds, sunflower seeds and almonds)
¾ cup (6 fl oz/175 ml) filtered water

Preheat the oven to 120°C/250°F.

Place all the ingredients except for the flax meal and water in the bowl of a food processor or blender and process until coarse. Transfer to a mixing bowl. Add the flax meal, stir through, then add the water a little at a time until it forms a dough-like mixture.

Turn out onto a baking sheet lined with baking paper and spread evenly. Place another sheet of baking paper on top, then roll over with a rolling pin until ¼ in (0.5 cm) thick.

Bake for 20–30 minutes until crispy. Cut into crisp bread squares with a pizza cutter. Keep in a sealed container into a dry place.

Cheesy Kale Crisp Bread

Cutting out cheese is rewarding to the body, and you'll soon notice the difference. This crisp bread offers a cheesy taste with added nutritional value. Serve with dips, salad or soup.

Serves 6–8

2 cups (5 oz/140 g) kale, washed and dried
1 cup (5 oz/150 g) flax meal (ground linseeds)
2 cups (7 oz/200 g) almond meal (ground almonds)
¾ cup (3 oz/90 g) nutritional (savoury) yeast
¼ teaspoon chilli powder
1 teaspoon paprika
¼ teaspoon Himalayan pink salt or Celtic sea salt
1 cup (8 fl oz/250 ml) water

Add all the ingredients to the bowl of a food processor or blender and blend until it forms a dough-like texture.

On Teflex or baking paper, press out the mixture to the edges. Place another sheet of baking paper on top, and roll over it using a rolling pin until smooth and flat, about ¼ in (0.5 cm) thick.

Dehydrate at 115°C/240°F for 2 hours. Cut with a pizza cutter into crisp bread squares.

Raw Zucchini Crisp Bread

This is a great gluten-free, dairy-free snack, that will energise your body. Serve with fresh hummus, or spread mashed avocado on top.

Serves 6–8

1 cup (4 oz/115 g) almonds
1 cup (5 oz/150 g) mixed sunflower and pumpkin seeds
2 tablespoons chia seeds
1 large zucchini (courgette), grated (shredded)
1 tablespoon olive oil
¼ teaspoon Himalayan pink salt or Celtic sea salt
1 teaspoon cumin
1 teaspoon oregano

Process the nuts in the bowl of a food processor or blender until fine. Add all of the other ingredients. The zucchini makes the mixture very moist and workable. Tip out the mixture onto a baking sheet lined with baking paper. Press out to the edges, then place another sheet of baking paper on top and roll over using a rolling pin until thin and smooth. Transfer to the tray of a dehydrator.

Dehydrate at 115°C/240°F for 3 hours, or bake in the oven for 1 hour at 95°C/200°F, turn off the oven and allow the crisp bread to dry overnight in a closed oven.

Quinoa Chia Seed Bread

This grainy seed bread is nutritious and filling. Top with salad and a dip.

Makes 1 loaf

2 tablespoon lecithin granules
¼ cup (1 oz/30 g) quinoa flour
¼ cup (1 oz/30 g) millet flour
¾ teaspoon Himalayan pink salt or Celtic sea salt
1 teaspoon nutritional (savoury) yeast
½ cup (2½ oz/75 g) chia seeds
1 tablespoon Starter (see Sourdough recipe)
1½ tablespoons honey
¾ cup (6 fl oz/175 ml) warm water

Add all the dry ingredients to a large bowl and mix to combine. Add the starter, honey and water, and knead well. You may have to use a little more dry flour to form your dough into a loaf.

Shape into dinner rolls and dehydrate for 8 hours at 115°C/240°F, or make one loaf and bake in the oven at 115°C/240°F for 1 hour.

Barbecue Crisp Bread

If you loved barbecue crisps in your youth, then you'll love this crisp bread to snack on with your favourite Raw food dip.

Serves 6–8

2 cups (8 oz/225 g) buckwheat flour
1 cup (4 oz/115 g) quinoa flour
1 cup (3½ oz/100 g) amaranth
1 teaspoon paprika
¼ teaspoon chilli flakes
½ teaspoon Himalayan pink salt or Celtic sea salt
2 tablespoons olive oil
⅓ cup (2½ fl oz/75 ml) warm filtered water

Blend all the dry ingredients in the bowl of a food processor or blender, then add the oil and blend again to combine. Add the water slowly, and use more, if needed, to form a dough-like consistency. Tip out onto baking paper, cover with another sheet of baking paper and use a rolling pin to roll over the dough until it is the thickness of a crisp bread.

Dehydrate for 3–4 hours at 115°C/240°F, or bake on very low heat, in the oven until dry, about 1 hour. Use a pizza cutter to cut into neat squares, ready for dipping.

Quinoa and Kale Crisp Bread

Similar to the kale crisp bread, this recipe offers more protein with a nutty taste and grainy texture. A great bread to use as an open sandwich filled with fresh salad and herbs.

Serves 6–8

1 cup (2¼ oz/65 g) kale
½ cup fresh basil
1 teaspoon cumin
1 teaspoon olive oil
½ teaspoon Himalayan pink salt or Celtic sea salt
1 teaspoon oregano
½ cup (2½ oz/75 g) sunflower seeds
2 cups (8 oz/225 g) LSA meal (mixed ground linseeds, sunflower seeds and almonds)
⅓ cup (2½ fl oz/75 ml) warm water
1 cup (6½ oz/185 g) cooked quinoa (I use the dark seed)
Sliced avocado, mixed salad, hummus or jam, to serve

Process the kale, basil, cumin, oil, salt and oregano in the bowl of a food processor then tip into a large bowl.

Process the sunflower seeds just until they form fine crumbs, then add to the bowl with the kale mixture. Stir through the LSA and then add the water a little at a time, and mix between each addition until a dough forms. Stir in the quinoa.

Turn out onto a baking sheet lined with baking paper and press the mixture out to the edges. Place a sheet of baking paper on top, then roll over with a rolling pin until flat and ¼ in (0.5 cm) thick. Remove the top paper and transfer to the tray of a dehydrator.

Dehydrate for 2–3 hours, or bake in the oven at 100°C/210°F for 30 minutes. Be careful not overbake. If you don't have a dehydrator, bake for 10–15 minutes and then turn off the oven and leave for 30 minutes with the oven door shut. Cut with a pizza cutter into squares

Top with avocado, salad, hummus or a jam.

Raisin 'Toast'

Cinnamon is a beautiful and healing spice to add to your food. Studies have shown in can help to regulate blood sugar control. This is a great Sunday morning breakfast.

Serves 6–8

½ cup (2½ oz/75 g) sunflower seeds
1 tablespoon chia seeds
1 cup (4 oz/115 g) almonds
½ cup (2 oz/115 g) ground flax
½ apple
1 carrot
2 dates soaked in 1⅓ cups (2½ fl oz/75 ml) filtered water
½ cup puréed zucchini (courgette)
½ teaspoon cinnamon powder
½ cup (2½ oz/75 g) raisins
Hazelnut Butter, to serve (see recipe)

Put the sunflower and chia seeds in the bowl of a food processor and process until finely chopped. Tip into a bowl.

Put the almonds in the food processor and process until finely chopped, but do not over process. Tip in the bowl with the sunflower and chia seeds. Add the flax and stir to combine.

Process the apple and carrot in a food processor until puréed. Add the zucchini purée and stir together.

Blend the soaked dates to a paste with ⅓ cup (2½ fl oz/75 ml) of the water. Add to the purée and stir through. Stir the puréed ingredients into the nuts and seeds and stir well. Stir in the cinnamon and raisins.

Spread out on baking paper or Teflex to ¼ in (0.5 cm) thick and place on a dehydrator tray. Dehydrate for 1–2 hours at 145°C/295°F, then reduce the heat and continue to dehydrate at 115°C/240°F for 2 more hours. Flip the mixture onto the screen and peel off the baking sheet.

Continue to dehydrate for 4–6 more hours, or until dry but not hard. This bread should be a little soft.

Sourdough

Sourdoughs are made with 'starters' rather than yeast, following an ancient method. First, a live culture is made which, once 'alive', can be refreshed and replenished and kept alive for years. If you follow this method you'll never need to use yeast to make bread ever again. You need to allow 3–5 days to create the starter. The longer you leave it the better the taste of the bread.

Note: Only use nutritional (savoury) yeast at the beginning of making the starter process. Do not add additional yeast when you feed the starter.

For the Starter
3 cups (12 oz/330 g) gluten-free flour,
3 probiotic capsules, emptied of their powder
1 teaspoon nutritional (savoury) yeast
¼ teaspoon Himalayan pink salt or Celtic sea salt
3 cups (24 fl oz/750 ml filtered water

Mix all the dry ingredients in a large bowl, add the water, stir well and cover. Set aside at room temperature for 3–5 days. In that time, every morning and evening 'feed' the starter, with equal amounts of water and flour. I stir the starter, then add ½ cup (2 oz/60 g) gluten-free flour and ½ cup (4 fl oz/125 ml) filtered water, stir again, making sure to scrape down the sides of the bowl, then cover and leave at room temperature. The starter is ready to use when it starts to bubble and smell sour, usually 3–5 days.

When you make your loaf, take 1 cup of the starter for use in the loaf, but remember to replace it immediately with ½ cup (2 oz/60 g) of gluten-free flour and ½ cup (4 fl oz/125 ml) filtered water and stir it in as if you are refreshing or feeding the mix. Do not add additional yeast when you feed the starter.

If your starter has been refrigerated, remove from the refrigerator at least 24 hours before you want to use it. Replenish the starter every time you remove a cupful to make a loaf.

Starter Variation

2 cups (8 oz/225 g) flaxseed meal
1 cup (4 oz/115 g) almond meal
1 cup (3½ oz/110 g) quinoa flour
1 teaspoon nutritional (savoury) yeast
3 probiotic capsules, emptied of their powder
¼ teaspoon Himalayan pink salt or Celtic sea salt
4 cups (1¾ pints/1 litre) filtered water

Combine all the ingredients in a very large bowl. The starter will grow and needs room to expand. Cover and leave at room temperature for 24 hours.

After 24 hours, stir the starter well, then feed with ½ cup (4 fl oz/125 ml) filtered water and ½ cup (2 oz/60 g) gluten-free flour, making sure to scrape the bottom well. After the first two feedings, you can cut the amount of flour and water by 50 per cent. Repeat for a total of 3–5 feedings.

Continue to feed daily if left at room temperature, or every few days if refrigerated.

Freekeh Sourdough

Freekeh is a low glycaemic index product, roasted as green grains. It is high in fibre, and contains more fibre, protein, vitamins and minerals than rice because it's harvested while still young and green.

Serves 4

1 cup (3½ oz/100 g) quinoa flour
1 cup (3½ oz/100 g) freekeh flour
1 cup (3½ oz/100 g) almond flour
¼ teaspoon Himalayan pink salt or Celtic sea salt
1 cup Sourdough Starter (see recipe)
Pumpkin seeds, to decorate

Mix all the dry ingredients in a large bowl. Stir in the starter. Shape the loaf and bake or dehydrate overnight for at least 8 hours, or bake in the oven in a baking dish on low heat for 40–60 minutes.

Sourdough Loaf

I grind my own flax seeds into flax meal, almonds into almond meal, quinoa into quinoa flour and brown rice into brown rice flour to use as the flour for my sourdough bread. It's a quick and easy process using a high-powered blender. This bread is best eaten fresh and will only keep for 1–2 days.

For the Dry Ingredients
1 tablespoon quinoa flour
1 cup (3½ oz/100 g) spelt flour
1 cup (4 oz/115 g) flax meal
1 tablespoon dried onion flakes
2 teaspoons onion powder
¼ teaspoon Himalayan pink salt or Celtic sea salt

For the Wet Ingredients
1 cup Sourdough Starter (see recipe)
2 tablespoons honey
1 tablespoon lemon juice

For the Topping
Chia seeds
Dried onion flakes
Ground flax seeds
Coconut oil, for greasing

Mix all the dry ingredients in a large bowl. Add the wet ingredients and mix into a dough-like consistency. Shape into a loaf or dinner rolls.

Use coconut oil to grease the 'baking' dish. Set the dough on top, then sprinkle seeds over the loaf, and dehydrate overnight, or bake at 75–100°C/165–210°F for 1 hour, or until dehydrated.

Sourdough Banana and Date Loaf

This is a sweet bread that is perfect for snacking on.

Makes 1 loaf

1 ripe banana
1 teaspoon vanilla extract
1 teaspoon ground cinnamon powder
Juice of 1 mandarin
⅓ cup (1¼ oz/40 g) activated walnuts (see introduction)
4 fresh dates
1 cup Sourdough Starter (see recipe)
1 cup (3½ oz/100 g) freekeh flour
½ cup (1¾ oz/50 g) spelt flour
½ (1¾ oz/50 g) quinoa flour
⅓ cup (1½ oz/45 g) pumpkin seeds

Put the banana, vanilla, cinnamon, mandarin juice, walnuts and 2 of the dates in the bowl of a blender or food processor and pulse until just combined and the walnuts still have texture.

In another bowl, mix the starter with the flours and pumpkin seeds. Chop the two remaining dates and add those too.

Pour into a baking dish and bake at 75–100°C/165–210°F for 1 hour, or shape into 2 loaves and place on baking paper or Teflex, arranging the shapes to fit in the dehydrator. Dehydrate for 8–10 hours.

Raw Cinnamon Buns

It's still possible to have food that has the texture of bread on a Raw food diet. These buns are sweet and filling. You could serve them with high tea.

Makes 6

For the Buns

½ cup (1¾ oz/50 g) flax meal (ground linseeds)
1 cup (3½ oz/100 g) almond flour (I use dehydrated almond pulp left over from making almond milk)
½ cup (1¾ oz/50 g) pecans, finely chopped
½ cup (1¾ oz/50 g) spelt flakes
1 teaspoon ground cinnamon
3 dates, soaked in ½ cup (4 fl oz/125 ml) filtered water for 10 minutes
1 tablespoon chia mixed with ⅓ cup (2½ fl oz/75 ml) filtered water
1½ tablespoon olive oil
1 cup (8 fl oz/250 ml) filtered water

For the Filling

⅓ cup (2½ oz/75 g) almonds, soaked in filtered water for 3 hours
½ cup (1¾ oz/50 g) cashew nuts, soaked in filtered water for 3 hours
1 cup young coconut (the white part)
2 fresh dates blended with 3 tablespoons filtered water
½ teaspoon vanilla extract
⅓ cup (1¾ oz/50 g) raisins

For the Icing

½ cup (4 oz/115 g) cashew butter
2 tablespoons maple syrup (not Raw)
½ teaspoon ground cinnamon powder
3 teaspoons filtered water

To make the buns, combine the flax meal, almond flour, finely chopped pecans, spelt flakes and cinnamon in a large bowl.

In another bowl, combine the date paste, olive oil and water. Mix the wet ingredients into the dry ingredients.

Spread in a rectangle on baking paper or a sheet of Teflex to less than ½ in (1.25 cm) thick. Dehydrate at 145°C/290°F for 30 minutes. Peel off the paper and dehydrate at 115°C/240°F for another 20 minutes.

Meanwhile, prepare the filling. Tip the drained soaked almonds and cashews into the bowl of a food processor or blender and process with the coconut, dates and vanilla until smooth. Stir in the raisins.

To make the icing, mix all the ingredients together in a small bowl.

Place a bun on a serving plate. Spread with filling and roll up carefully like a bun shape, or spread on top and add icing. Serve with thawed frozen boysenberries.

Chapter Three

3 HEALTHY JUICES AND HEALING TEAS

Clean Green Kale Smoothie

Green smoothies are a hit in the Raw food world, and kale, the most nutritious of greens, provides large quantities of anti-oxidants and other beneficial nutrients.

Serves 2

1 pint (600 ml) water
1 cup (2¼ oz/65 g) kale, rinsed, dried and chopped
1 cup (1 oz/30 g) English spinach, rinsed, dried and chopped
1 banana, chopped
1 in (2.5 cm) ginger root
1 tablespoon chia seeds
Juice of ½ lemon

Pour the water into a blender or food processor, and add the remaining ingredients. Process or blend until smooth.

Store in glass preserving bottles and refrigerate for up to 48 hours.

Sweet Greens Juice

We normally associate greens with bitterness. However, the flavour of this vitamin and nutrient-packed juice may surprise you. It's great for energy and vitality.

Serves 3

3 large silver beet leaves, including stalk, chopped
3 kale, including stalk, chopped
1 large green apple, chopped
1 cup (6 oz/170 g) fresh pineapple, chopped
1 cucumber, chopped
1 zucchini (courgette), chopped
3 celery stalks, chopped
½ lemon, chopped
1 in (2.5 cm) 1 teaspoon fresh root ginger
1½ pints (900 ml) water

Tip all the ingredients into a blender and blend on low speed, then increase the speed to high and blend until smooth.

Store in airtight glass and consume within 48 hours.

To add extra nutrients to healing juices, blend 1 scoop of 7.2 greens powder with ½ pint (300 ml) water and mix with the juice.

Lean Green Juice

You can drink this juice slightly warm for easier digestion.

Serves 3

1 cup (2¼ oz/65 g) kale, chopped
2 celery stalks, chopped
½ cucumber, chopped
2 limes, skin removed, sliced
1 green apple, chopped
2 in (5 cm) root ginger, peeled
1½ pints (900 ml) filtered water

Tip all the ingredients into a blender and blend on low, then increase the speed to high and blend until smooth.

Store in airtight glass and consume within 48 hours.

Spinach Cocktail

The mint gives this smoothie a lovely refreshing taste. It is easy to digest and satisfying for a sweeter tooth.

1 cup (6 oz/170 g) fresh pineapple, cubed
3 fresh mint leaves
1 cup (1 oz/30 g) spinach leaves, chopped
1 cup ice cubes

Tip all the ingredients into a blender and blend on low speed, then increase the speed to high and blend until smooth.

Drink immediately for optimal nutrition. All smoothies and juices are best consumed immediately, although they will keep in a glass jar in the refrigerator for 48 hours. Shake well, before drinking.

Carrot, Ginger and Turmeric Juice

A great cleansing drink and immunity booster.

Serves 2

1 medium carrot, chopped
1 orange, including pith, chopped
½ apple, core included, chopped
1 in (2.5 cm) turmeric or 1 teaspoon turmeric powder
½ in (2.5 cm) fresh root ginger, peeled
1 cup ice cubes
1 cup (8 fl oz/250 ml) filtered water

Add all the ingredients to the blender and blend until smooth. Store in a glass container in the refrigerator.

Liver-Cleansing Turmeric Juice

Serves 2

Use the powdered spice or purchase fresh turmeric and prepare it as you would Raw ginger. It's a refreshing and uplifting juice.

2 turmeric roots, chopped
¼ pineapple, peeled and cubed
½ lemon, chopped
2 sprigs fresh mint
2 in (5 cm) fresh root ginger, peeled
2 cups (16 fl oz/500 ml) filtered water

Tip all the ingredients into a blender and blend at high speed for 2 minutes. Pour into a glass jug (pitcher) and store in the refrigerator.

Store in airtight glass and consume within 48 hours.

Celery and Ginger Lemon

The core of the apple is included in this juice. It's as nutritious as the apple flesh.

Serves 2

1 celery stalk, chopped
1 green apple, quartered
Juice of ½ lemon
1 in (2.5 cm) root ginger, peeled
1 slice fresh pineapple, cubed
1 pint (600 ml) filtered water

Tip all the ingredients into a high-speed blender, and process until smooth. Drink immediately or store in airtight glass containers and refrigerate.

Turmeric Juice

Soothing to the digestive system, this healing juice is uplifting.

Serves 2

2 pieces turmeric root, each 2–3 in (5–7.5 cm) long
1 lemon, peeled
⅓ pineapple, cubed
2 cups (16 fl oz/500 ml) filtered water

Blend all the ingredients in a blender until they form the consistency of juice. Strain through a mesh cloth or nut bag to collect pulp and give you a smoother juice. Strain through a mesh cloth or nut bag to collect pulp and give you a smoother juice. Decant into glass containers, seal and store in the refrigerator.

Cucumber Juice

This refreshing juice is a great weight-loss drink, and an immunity booster.

Serves 4

1 cucumber, chopped
3 mint leaves
1 lemon, chopped
1 in (2.5 cm) piece of root ginger, peeled
1½ pints (900 ml) filtered water

Tip all the ingredients into a blender and blend on low speed, then increase the speed to high and blend until smooth.

Drink immediately for optimal nutrition or store in a glass jar and keep refrigerated for up to 48 hours. Shake well, before drinking.

Beetroot Juice

This drink is a tonic for the liver. Traditionally, beetroot is also a tonic for the skin and kidneys. It helps ward against fatigue and eye problems. It has inflammatory properties.

Serves 8

2 beetroots (beet), quartered
½ cup beet leaves, chopped
½ teaspoon Himalayan pink salt or Celtic sea salt
1 pint 7 fl oz (800 ml) filtered water
2 large carrots, chopped
1 stalk celery, chopped
1 in (2.5 cm) fresh root ginger, peeled

Soak the beetroot in a bowl with the salt and water and leave to soak overnight. The next day, discard the beetroot. Tip the liquid into a blender. Add the carrots, celery and ginger. Blend until smooth. Store in a large airtight jar in the refrigerator. Keep for 48 hours.

Pineapple and Ginger Juice

This healthy and healing juice tastes sweet and spicy. It's great for weight loss and to cleanse the digestive system.

Serves 4

1 pineapple, peel discarded and flesh cubed
1 in (2.5 cm) fresh root ginger, peeled
Juice of 1 lemon
1 pint 3½ fl oz (700 ml) filtered water
1 cup ice cubes

Tip all the ingredients into a blender and blend at high speed for 2 minutes. Pour into a glass jug (pitcher) and store in the refrigerator for up to 48 hours

Frozen Strawberry and Grape Juice

Freeze a glut of grapes to use in this delicious juice. With the addition of strawberries, this is a juice to satisfy a sweet craving.

Serves 2

1 cup (4 oz/115 g) strawberries, frozen
1 cup (4 oz/115 g) green grapes, with or without seeds, frozen or thawed
1 cup (4 oz/115 g) red grapes, with or without seeds
½ cup ice cubes

Blend all the ingredients in a blender at high speed until liquid. Pour into a glass jug (pitcher) and store in the refrigerator for up to 48 hours

Celery and Grape Juice

Celery is a wonderful source of vitamin C. Add it to your daily diet to benefit from its nutritional value. Celery has a distinct taste. The addition of lemon juice and grapes add a sweet tang.

Serves 4

4 large celery stalks, chopped
1 cup (4 oz/115 g) frozen grapes
1 in (2.5 cm) fresh root ginger, peeled
Juice of ½ lemon
1 pint (600 ml) water

Blend all the ingredients in a blender at high speed until liquid. Pour in glass jars and store in the refrigerator.

Apple Cider Refresher

This is a refreshing cider that helps maintain a healthy pH level in the body. This drink brings the body into alkaline state and can help detoxify the liver, gut flora and aid digestion.

Serves 2

2 oranges, including the pith, chopped
2 tablespoons apple cider
½ apple, chopped
½ cup (3 oz/85 g) fresh pineapple, cubed
½ teaspoon honey (optional)
1 cup ice cubes

Tip all the ingredients into a blender and blend on low speed, then increase the speed to high and blend until smooth.

Turmeric, Ginger and Honey Tea

This is my favourite night-time drink. Turmeric has phenomenal healing powers so this is a drink you can enjoy daily.

2 in (5 cm) piece of turmeric, grated (shredded)
1 in (2.5 cm) piece of root ginger, grated (shredded)
Juice of ½ lemon
1 teaspoon honey

Tip the turmeric and ginger into the teapot. Add the lemon and honey, then pour over hot, but not boiling, filtered water and allow to brew for 5 minutes before pouring, or blend all the ingredients with cooled water and use as a concentrate adding boiling water to make the drink – so that you get the intense ginger and turmeric honey flavour.

Ginger, Lemon and Honey Tea

A lovely calming, healing drink that is great for the digestive system.

2 in (5 cm) piece of root ginger, grated (shredded)
Juice of 1 lemon
1 teaspoon honey

Add the grated ginger root to a teapot with the lemon and honey. Pour over hot, but not boiling, filtered water and allow to brew for 5 minutes before pouring.

Chia Tea

Chia tea is naturally healing. It contains a blend of beneficial spices such as cinnamon to aid inflammation, star anise to aid digestion, cloves to settle the stomach and honey to keep the skin nourished. It is packed with anti-oxidants to help combat free radicals and leave you feeling balanced and energised.

3 cardamom pods
1 star anise
2 cloves
1 in (2.5 cm) fresh root ginger
1 stick cinnamon
¼ teaspoon Himalayan pink salt or Celtic sea salt
¼ teaspoon cinnamon powder
1 teaspoon black Ceylon tea
Hot water
1 teaspoon honey, to serve
Almond milk, to serve (see recipe)

Crush the cardamom pods, star anise and cloves with a pestle and mortar to release the flavour.

Pour all the spices into the teapot and pour on boiling water. Leave to brew for 5 minutes, then pour through a strainer.

Drink black or with almond milk and sweetened with honey.

Turmeric and Black Peppercorn Tea

Black peppercorns add heat to this warming drink. The turmeric adds a pleasing yellow colour.

1¾ pints (1 litre) filtered water
¾ teaspoon cumin seeds
1 teaspoon coriander seeds
1 in (2.5 cm) fresh root ginger, peeled
½ teaspoon black peppercorns
3 cloves
1 cinnamon shard

Put all the ingredients in a large pan and bring to the boil. Boil for 7 minutes, then set aside to steep for another 5 minutes. Strain and pour into tea cups, or add all ingredients to the blender with 16 fl oz (500 ml) water, blend well and use this to add to boiling water for a more concentrated flavour.

Chapter Four

4 BREAKFAST DISHES AND FRUIT SMOOTHIES

Raw Muesli

A great way to start the day, this cereal is full of nutritious and healthy ingredients.

Serves 4

⅓ cup (1¾ oz/50 g) raisins
1/3 cup (1¼ oz/40 g) activated almonds (see recipe)
1/3 cup (1¼ oz/40 g) goji berries
⅓ cup (1¾ oz/50 g) sunflower seeds
⅓ cup (1½ oz/45 g) pumpkin seeds
⅓ cup (2½ oz/75 g) dried apricots, chopped
1 cup (3¼ oz/90 g) spelt oats
½ cup (2 oz/60 g) strawberries, chopped, to serve
½ cup (2 oz/60 g) blueberries, to serve
½ cup (4 fl oz/125 g) coconut kefir yogurt, to serve
2 tablespoons chia seeds, for topping

To make the basic muesli mix, combine the raisins, almonds, goji berries, seeds, dried apricots and oats together in a large container, then divide between breakfast bowls. Top with strawberries and blueberries and serve with coconut kefir yogurt. Scatter over the chia seeds

Raw **Granola**

This nutty and fruity cereal is packed with nutritional goodness. You can make this recipe up and store it in the refrigerator and enjoy in small snacks throughout the day or eat for breakfast, with added fresh fruit.

Serves 8

1 apple, peeled, cored and chopped
2 tablespoons chia
2 teaspoons ground cinnamon
¼ teaspoon pink Himalayan or Celtic sea salt
Juice of 2 mandarins
1 tablespoon mandarin zest
1 tablespoon lemon zest
1 cup (4 oz/115 g) almonds, soaked in water for 3–8 hours
1 cup (4 oz/115 g) walnuts, soaked in water for 3–8 hours
½ cup (2½ oz/70 g) pumpkin seeds
½ cup (2½ oz/75 g) sunflower seeds
1 cup (4 oz/115 g) cranberries
Sliced bananas, to serve
Flaxseed oil, to drizzle

Put the apple, 1 tablespoon of chia seeds, the cinnamon, salt, mandarin juice and zests in the bowl of a food processor and blend until chunky. Be careful not to over-blend the mixture. Tip into a bowl.

Process the nuts until chunky, then add to the bowl with the chia mixture. Add the seeds, cranberries and remaining chia seeds and mix together until well combined. Store, covered, in the refrigerator to allow the flavours to blend overnight.

Divide between breakfast bowls and serve with sliced banana and drizzle flaxseed oil over the top.

Seedy Breaky

Make up a batch of this seed mix and store in glass containers for those busy mornings when you're short of time.

Serves 3

1 cup (5 oz/140 g) pumpkin seeds
¼ cup 1½ oz/40 g) chia seeds
⅓ cup (1¾ oz/50 g) sunflower seeds
⅓ cup buckwheat flakes
2 tablespoons desiccated (dry unsweetened shredded) coconut
⅓ cup (1¼ oz/40 g) goji berries
⅓ cup (1¾ oz/50 g) raisins
Fresh fruit, such as strawberries or blueberries, to serve
½ banana, to serve
2 oz (60 g) raisins

Combine all the seeds, coconut and goji berries in a large airtight container and mix until well combined.

Tip ¼ cup of the seed mix into a breakfast bowl, top with chopped fruit and raisins. Serve with pineapple and blueberries.

Pancakes

Gluten-free pancakes are becoming popular now that more people are being choosing a wheat-free diet. For those following a Raw lifestyle it means you can still enjoy this treat with family and friends.

Serves 2

1 cup (8 fl oz/250 ml) almond milk mixed with 1 tablespoon chia seeds
1 ripe banana, sliced
1 fresh date, sliced
¼ teaspoon Himalayan pink salt or Celtic sea salt
1 teaspoon cinnamon
½ teaspoon vanilla extract
1 cup (4 oz/115 g) coconut flour
½ cup (1¾ oz/50 g) almond flour
Banana, chocolate sauce and coconut kefir yogurt, to serve

Mix the cup of almond milk with the chia seeds in a bowl and set aside for 5 minutes to become glutinous.

Blend the sliced banana, sliced date, salt, cinnamon and vanilla extract together in a large bowl. Slowly add the almond milk and chia seed mixture, while mixing. Fold in the flour, stir in more almond milk until a pancake batter consistency is reached.

Dehydrate on silicone sheets for 4 hours, or bake in the oven at a low temperature. Serve with fresh banana slices, chocolate sauce and kefir yogurt.

Blueberry Pancakes

These blueberry pancakes are fun to make. Living a **Raw** lifestyle is about creating different textures to keep your meals interesting and satisfying. These dehydrate really well.

Serves 6–8

1 ripe banana, sliced
1 cup (4 oz/115 g) pecans, soaked in filtered water for 8 hours
1 cup (4 oz/115 g) pine nuts
½ cup (4 fl oz/125 ml) filtered water
1 fresh date
1 teaspoon vanilla extract
¼ teaspoon Himalayan pink salt or Celtic sea salt
2 tablespoons maple syrup, plus extra to serve
¾ cup (3 oz/85 g) blueberries, plus extra to serve

Put the banana, pecans, pine nuts, water, date, vanilla, salt and maple syrup in the bowl of a blender or processor and blend until smooth. Stir the blueberries through the batter then spread into 5 in (12.5 cm) rounds on sheets of silicone.

Dehydrate for 24–48 hours. Serve warm with maple syrup and fresh blueberries.

Fresh Fruit Lecithin, Seeds and Kefir Yogurt

Keeping life simple is a part of the Raw food lifestyle. I've added a few lecithin granules to this fruit salad for extra nutrients.

Serves 1

½ cup (3 oz/85 g) fresh pineapple, finely sliced
⅓ cup (1¾ oz/50 g) watermelon, chopped
½ apple, finely sliced
1 strawberry, sliced
⅓ cup (1¼ oz/35 g) blueberries
⅓ cup (1¼ oz/35 g) frozen mixed berries, thawed
2 tablespoons kefir yogurt
Honey, to drizzle
2 tablespoons mixed seeds and lecithin granules

Arrange the fruit on a plate, drizzle over the kefir yogurt and honey. Scatter the mixed seeds and lecithin granules on top.

Turmeric Fruit Purée

This is a wonderful condiment or purée to add to breakfast, salads or desserts.

Serves 2

1 banana, frozen
½ fresh mango, cubed
¼ fresh pineapple, cubed
3 in (7.5 cm) turmeric root
1 tablespoon chia seeds
½ cup Raw Muesli (see recipe)

Tip the banana, mango, pineapple, turmeric and chia seeds into the bowl of a blender and process until puréed.

Divide the **Raw** muesli between breakfast dishes, top with the blended fruit purée.

Tips for great-tasting smoothies

Enjoy smoothies at room temperature, rather than cold.
Add a pinch of turmeric and ginger and a squeeze of lemon to aid digestion.
Add a little coconut oil to offset any dry or rough qualities of the vegetables.
Try a smoothie without fruit or use avocado or ripe bananas that takes a little longer to digest.

Banana and Coconut Smoothie

This smoothie offers a stunning combination of flavours and is filling and satisfying too. Banana is packed with potassium and coconut water helps to keep you hydrated. The pineapple can aid digestion and provides a pleasant sweet taste.

Serves 1

1 banana, sliced, reserve a few slices to decorate
⅓ cup (2½ fl oz/75 ml) coconut water
¼ cup (1½ oz/45 g) fresh pineapple
1 teaspoon lecithin granules
¼ cup (2 fl oz/60 ml) Almond Milk (see recipe)
1 cup ice cubes

Tip all the ingredients into the bowl of a food processor or blender and blend at high speed until smooth. Drink immediately or store in the refrigerator, covered, for up to 48 hours.

Peach and Coconut Smoothie

Peaches are beautiful in smoothies and provide a natural sweet taste. They are tasty when mixed with banana and coconut.

Serves 2

½ cup (2 oz/60 g) strawberries, fresh or frozen
½ banana, sliced
1 tablespoon coconut oil
¼ cup (1½ oz/45 g) fresh pineapple, cubed
¼ cup (2 fl oz/60 ml) Almond Milk (see recipe)
1 cup ice cubes
1 cup peach slices or 2 medium peaches, sliced
⅓ cup (2½ fl oz/75 ml) coconut water

Tip all the ingredients into the bowl of a food processor or blender and blend at speed until smooth.

Lucia's Slushy Pineapple Coconut

Pineapple and coconut are perfect to serve for breakfast on a hot summer's morning.

Serves 2

1 cup (8 fl oz/250 ml) pineapple juice
½ cup ice cubes
½ banana, sliced
½ cup (3 oz/85 g) fresh pineapple
½ cup coconut meat

Blend the pineapple juice, ice and banana together until a slushy texture is formed. Add the pineapple and coconut milk and blend until smooth and the fruit is well mixed.

Coconut, Mango and Kiwi Juice

This is one of my favourite smoothies; the mix of the kiwi, spinach and coconut is stunning. I love the vivid green colour this smoothie has. It is a high-powered, nutrient-based smoothie that will keep you feeling full for hours.

Serves 1

½–1 cup (4–8 fl oz/125–250 ml) coconut water
Meat from 1 green coconut, chopped
1 mango, flesh chopped
1 kiwi fruit, chopped
2 cups (2 oz/60 g) fresh baby spinach (or other leafy green)

Tip all the ingredients into the bowl of a food processor or blender and blend at high speed until smooth.

Coconut and Peach Smoothie

Coconut mixed with sweet peach tastes stunning. Keeping your diet varied and seasonal is the key to ensuring you get a wide range of nutrients, vitamins and minerals.

Serves 1

½–1 cup (4–8 fl oz/125–250 ml) coconut water
Meat from 1 green coconut, chopped
1 medium to large peach, chopped

Tip all the ingredients into the bowl of a food processor or blender and blend at high speed until smooth.

Milli's Summer Dream

I have one daughter who loves sugar, so it's an ongoing challenge to create **Raw**, healthy and tasty recipes to satisfy her sweet tooth. If you are the same, then raspberries and mango mixed together give a sweet summery taste. Mangoes are a great alkaline food that benefit people who suffer from indigestion. They are also high in iron.

Serves 2

1 cup (3½ oz/100 g) fresh mango, cubed
1 cup (4½ oz/130 g) frozen raspberries
½–1 cup (4–8 fl oz/125–250 ml) coconut water
I cup ice cubes

Tip all the ingredients into the bowl of a food processor or blender, and blend at high speed until smooth.

Chapter Five

SOUPS AND DIPS

5

Sweet Beetroot Soup

This soup is sweet and visually beautiful. Dark red beetroot is high in anti-oxidants, so this soup promotes anti-ageing, helping prevent illness. Bottle this soup and it will keep for 48 hours. Warm your plate if you prefer a warm soup.

Serves 2

2 cups (16 fl oz/500 ml) filtered water, at room temperature
2 beetroots (beets), peeled
2 tomatoes
8 strawberries
5 shallots

Put all the ingredients into the bowl of a food processor or blender. Set the blender to low speed and gradually increase it to high speed. You may have to stop the power and scrape down the ingredients before restarting it. Blend for 4–6 minutes, or until the soup reaches the desired temperature.

Vegetable stock

1 carrot, peeled and chopped
1 onion, peeled and chopped
2 celery sticks, peeled and chopped
$1/4$ teaspoon cayenne pepper
$1/4$ teaspoon chilli
$1/4$ teaspoon Himalayan pink salt or Celtic sea salt
$1/4$ teaspoon cracked pepper

To make your own vegetable stock, add all the ingredients to a large pan with 1¾ pints (1 litre) of filtered water and heat gently. Make sure you do not boil the vegetables.

Turmeric Cauliflower Soup

Research shows turmeric has anti-inflammatory properties. It is healing for joints and arthritis. Make turmeric part of your life for health and longevity.

Serves 4

1 medium cauliflower, chopped into florets
2 cups (16 fl oz/500 ml) filtered water
Juice of 1 lemon
2½ tablespoons gluten-free tamari soy sauce
½ teaspoon turmeric
Chopped parsley, to garnish
¼ teaspoon Himalayan pink salt or Celtic sea salt
Cracked black pepper, to taste

Add all the ingredients to the bowl of a blender of food processor and blend until smooth. If you'd like a thinner texture, add a little more water.

Tomato and Basil Soup

Packed with flavour, this soup is both filling satisfying. It has a creamy quality from the addition of Brazil nut milk, which adds extra nutrients. If you are making this dish for one person then halve the recipe and store some in a glass jar for the next day.

Serves 4

3 large tomatoes, sliced or whole, dehydrated for 5 hours
¼ cup (2 fl oz/60 ml) olive oil
1 tablespoon dried oregano
¼ teaspoon Himalayan pink salt or Celtic sea salt
¼ teaspoon cracked black pepper
1 teaspoon dried rosemary
1 teaspoon dried basil
2 cups (16 fl oz/500 ml) filtered water
¼ Spanish (Bermuda) onion
½ cup (4 fl oz/125 ml) Brazil Nut Milk (see recipe)

In the bowl of a blender process all the ingredients until smooth. Heat the serving bowls before pouring in the soup.

Sweet Corn Soup

Corn is high in fibre and anti-oxidants. It is a rich source of vitamins A, B, E and many minerals, making it good for the digestive system. The anti-oxidants present in corn also act as anti-carcinogenic agents.

Serves 4

2 fresh corn on the cob, corn removed
½ carrot
⅓ Spanish (Bermuda) onion
1 celery stick
¼ cup (1½ oz/45 g) quinoa
16 fl oz (500 ml) vegetable stock
¼ teaspoon Himalayan pink salt or Celtic sea salt

Add all the ingredients to the bowl of a blender with 16 fl oz (500 ml) filtered water and process until smooth.

Warm the soup plate before serving. Cold soups are best served and consumed immediately and at room temperature for optimum nutrition and taste.

Zucchini Soup

This healing and energising soup is very low in calories making it a great choice for weight loss.

Serves 2

3 zucchini (courgettes), peeled
Juice of 1 lemon
⅓ cup (2½ fl oz/75 ml) olive oil
¼ teaspoon Himalayan pink salt or Celtic sea salt
1 teaspoon ground ginger
1 teaspoon onion, diced
1 teaspoon maple syrup
1 teaspoon cumin
1 cup (8 fl oz/250 ml) filtered water
1 tablespoon chia seeds
Coriander (cilantro), to garnish
Cracked black pepper, to taste

Blend all the ingredients in the bowl of a blender until smooth. Garnish with coriander and cracked black pepper to taste.

Healing Soup

Packed with greens and gentle on the digestive system, this recipe makes enough for you to drink over
3 days to give your body a gentle cleanse. It is easily digested and a great way to detoxify your body from packaged or processed foods. It's high in iron because of the dark leafy greens. This is a warm soup not a Raw soup. Store bottled in the refrigerator and use within a week.

Serves 6–8

4 cups (1¾ pints/1 litre) filtered water
4 medium zucchini (courgettes), finely chopped
3 celery stalks, leaves removed, finely chopped
1 cup (5 oz/150 g) broccoli
3 kale leaves
1 large bunch fresh parsley, chopped
3 medium tomatoes, finely chopped
3 garlic cloves, finely chopped
2 teaspoons sea salt
1 teaspoon dried thyme
1 teaspoon dried rosemary
1 teaspoon dried oregano

Add all of the ingredients to a large stock pan or sauté pot. Bring to a gentle boil, then lower the heat, cover, and simmer gently for 30 minutes. Serve warm.

Vegetable Soup

Cabbage, the main vegetable in this dish, is rich in beta-carotene. The more foods you eat that are rich in vitamins, minerals, anti-oxidants and beta-carotene, the healthier you will feel.

Serves 4–6

3 cups (1 lb 2 oz/500 g) tomatoes
½ medium cabbage, quartered
1 cup (5 oz/140 g) carrots
2 celery stalks, halved
1 medium onion, quartered
⅓–⅔ oz (10–20 g) frozen spinach
4 cups (1¾ pints/1 litre) vegetable stock
⅛ teaspoon white pepper
¼ teaspoon rosemary
1 small clove garlic (optional)

Put all of the ingredients in the bowl of a blender and process until smooth. Warm in a large pan set over medium heat.

Avocado Green Soup

Avocados are fabulously healthy. They contain 25 essential nutrients including vitamins A, B, C, E and K, copper, iron, phosphorus, magnesium and potassium. They also contain fibre and protein.

Serves 2

1 avocado, peeled, seed removed and flesh chopped
1 tablespoon Spanish (Bermuda) onion, diced
1 tomato
1 cucumber
Juice of 1 lemon
2 basil leaves
1 tablespoon continental parsley
1 spinach leaf
1 teaspoon almond oil or any cold-pressed oil
½ teaspoon Himalayan pink salt or Celtic sea salt
Fresh vegetable sticks, to serve

Put all the ingredients in the bowl of a blender or food processor and blend until smooth. Decant into a small bowl and serve as a dip for fresh vegetables.

Cumin and Chia Hummus

Chickpeas are naturally low in fat and high in fibre. Eating them regularly can help reduce the risk of developing type 2 diabetes.

Makes 2 cups

2 cups (1 lb 2 oz/500 g) dried chickpeas, soaked overnight in water
1 garlic clove
1 teaspoon cumin
4 tablespoons sesame seeds
1 tablespoon chia seeds
1 tablespoon olive oil
¼ cup (2 fl oz/60 ml) lemon juice

Place all the ingredients in the bowl of a food processor and blender or blend at high speed for 3 minutes, or until smooth. Store covered in the refrigerator for up to 3 days

Spinach and Kale Dip

Dark green vegetables help detoxify your body and keep your liver healthy. Serve with gluten-free crisp breads or with Raw vegetable sticks.

Makes 4 cups

1 cup (8 oz/225 g) dried chickpeas, soaked overnight in water
1 cup (4 oz/115 g) soaked almonds, skin removed
1 cup (1 oz/30 g) spinach leaves
1 cup (2¼ oz/65 g) kale
¼ cup (1½ oz/40 g) onion
1 small garlic clove
1 teaspoon cumin
Juice of 1 lemon
Himalayan pink salt or Celtic sea salt, to taste

Place all the ingredients in the bowl of a blender or processor, stopping occasionally to scrape down the sides, and blend to a smooth consistency. Do not over mix. Store covered in the refrigerator for up to 3 days.

Avocado Dip

Avocados are full of healing benefits. As a fruit they are the best source of vitamin E, helping protect against disease and maintain overall health.

Makes 1½ cups

2 ripe avocados
1 teaspoon Himalayan pink salt or Celtic sea salt
2 tablespoons lemon juice
¼ cup (1½ oz/40 g) onion
1 medium tomato
½ cup fresh cilantro (coriander)

Blend all of ingredients in the bowl of a food processor or blender on medium speed until smooth. Store covered in the refrigerator for up to 3 days.

Raw Hummus

Chickpeas have a delicious nutty taste and are nutritious and filling. They're versatile too. Make them into hummus or dips, sprinkle over salads or soak, dehydrate and mill into chickpea flour.

Serves 4

1 cup (7 oz/200 g) dried chickpeas, soaked in water overnight
1 tablespoon tahini
Juice of ½ lemon
½ garlic clove
3 tablespoons olive oil
½ teaspoon Himalayan pink salt or Celtic sea salt

Drain and rinse the chickpeas. Add all the ingredients to the bowl of a blender or food processor. Start on low speed and gradually increase to high speed. Blend well, for 4–5 minutes until creamy and smooth. If the hummus is too thick, add 1 tablespoon of water or olive oil. Store in a glass jar in the refrigerator for 3 days.

Coriander Salsa

Coriander is known to lower blood sugar by stimulating the secretion of insulin. It's also great for the skin.

Makes 2 cups

¼ cup fresh coriander (cilantro)
½ Spanish (Bermuda) onion
1 teaspoon lemon juice
1 tablespoon olive oil
6 ripe tomatoes, quartered
1 jalapeño pepper
1 teaspoon Himalayan pink salt or Celtic sea salt
Fresh vegetable sticks, to serve

Add all the ingredients to the bowl of a processor or blender. Blend for a approximately 10 seconds until well mixed but not necessarily smooth.

Spicy Jalapeño Salsa

Served with salads, this salsa adds an Italian flavour, or serve as a dressing with spiralised zucchini.

Makes 5 cups

2 cups ripe tomatoes
1 large jalapeño pepper
3 green chillies, canned
2 tablespoons tomato paste
½ cup fresh coriander (cilantro)
½ teaspoon Himalayan pink salt or Celtic sea salt
1 tablespoon olive oil (optional)

Add all the ingredients to the bowl of a processor or blender. Blend for approximately 10 seconds

Thai Chia Dressing

This dressing imparts Thai flavour and is great to serve with sprouted grains and vegetables or with Raw zucchini noodles and salad.

Makes 2 cups

½ cup (4 fl oz/125 ml) sesame oil
½ cup (4 fl oz/125 ml) soy sauce
½ cup (4 fl oz/125 ml) olive oil
½ cup (4 fl oz/125 ml) lime juice
1 tablespoon maple syrup
2 Thai chillies or 1½ teaspoons chilli flakes
1 teaspoon Himalayan pink salt or Celtic sea salt
¼ cup (1 oz/30 g) cashew nuts

Blend all ingredients until smooth.

Cashew Chia Cream

Serve with spiralised zucchini as a pasta-style dressing. Add sun-dried tomatoes and olives too, if you like.

Makes 1 cup

1 cup (4 oz/115 g) cashew nuts, soaked in filtered water for 1–2 hours
Juice of 1 lemon
¼ teaspoon Himalayan pink salt or Celtic sea salt
1 teaspoon maple syrup or Raw honey
1 tablespoon olive oil
¼ cup (2 fl oz/60 ml) filtered water

Blend all ingredients for 5 minutes or until smooth and creamy.

Serve with **Raw** vegetable batons, such as celery, carrot and capsicum, or use as a dip on crackers. If liked, add more water and use it as a dressing for salads.

Mango and Coriander Chutney

Great for dips or spreads, or as a dressing for salad.

Makes 1 cup

2 cups mango, chopped
1 cup (3 oz/85 g) fresh coconut meat
¼ teaspoon cayenne pepper
¼ teaspoon chilli flakes
¼ teaspoon Himalayan pink salt or Celtic sea salt
¼ cup coriander (cilantro), roughly chopped

Blend for 10 seconds in the blender, but do not over-process.

Avocado Dip and Tomato Salsa

Serve as a light snack or as part of a tapas-style dinner party.

Makes 1 cup

1 avocado, peeled, seed removed and flesh mashed
1 cup (5 oz/140 g) carrots, cut into batons
½ bunch celery, cut into batons
½ red capsicum (bell pepper), sliced
1 cup (5 oz/150 g) broccoli, sliced

For the Salsa Dip
4 Roma tomatoes
½ cup fresh basil
1 tablespoon balsamic vinegar
Juice of ½ lemon
¼ teaspoon chilli flakes
¼ teaspoon Himalayan pink salt or Celtic sea salt

To make the salsa dip, blend all the ingredients in the bowl of a food processor or blender. Mash the avocado flesh in a bowl, top with the salsa. Arrange the vegetables around the bowl of the salsa dip.

Chapter Six
6 LIGHT MEALS
AND SALADS

Nori Salad

Nori has a high protein content. It's rich in minerals too, especially iodine, calcium, iron and magnesium.

Serves 1–2

1 ripe avocado, peeled, seed removed and flesh chopped
2 small cucumbers, halved and chopped
1 red capsicum (bell pepper), finely chopped
½ cup sprouted seeds
½ cup fresh coriander (cilantro), finely chopped
1 nori sheet, cut into bite-size pieces
1 tablespoon chia seeds, to garnish

For the Dressing
1 tablespoon ginger root, finely grated (shredded)
1 tablespoon gluten-free tamari soy sauce
Juice of 1 lemon

To make the salad, mix the avocado, cucumbers, red capsicum, sprouts, coriander and strips of nori together in a bowl.

To make the dressing, mix the ingredients together in a small bowl. Tip the salad dressing over the salad and scatter chia seeds on top to garnish.

Macadamia Crumble

Mix these ingredients together. They taste great scattered on top of salads.

½ cup (2 oz/60 g) macadamia nuts
1 tablespoon almond milk
Himalayan pink salt or Celtic sea salt, to taste

Zucchini Pasta and Rocket Pesto

Zucchini is a nutritious and healing vegetable. It is great for weight loss and easy to eat Raw. Try this recipe to replace the pasta and gluten in your diet. The texture is beautiful and very filling and satisfying. When you remove heavy foods from your diet, your energy levels will rise.

Serves 2

1 cup (6 oz/150 g) cherry tomatoes, quartered
Sourdough, to serve (see recipe)
Balsamic vinegar, to serve

For the Pesto
1 cup rocket (arugula)
1 cup fresh basil
½ cup (2 oz/60 g) pistachio nuts, soaked in water for 2 hours
2 tablespoons olive oil
Juice of ½ lemon
½ teaspoon garlic powder
½ teaspoon Himalayan pink salt or Celtic sea salt
¼ teaspoon cracked black pepper
2 zucchini (courgettes)

For the Pasta
2 zucchini (courgettes)

Place all ingredients in a food processor and blend until chunky.

To make the pasta, spiralise the zucchini. Arrange in a large serving bowl, mix in the pesto, and add the cherry tomatoes.

Serve with gluten-free sourdough and balsamic vinegar.

Raw Sprouted Salad Sandwich with Mango and Coriander Dressing

You can't beat this crisp bread with its fresh salad and veggies. It tastes clean, crisp and very satisfying. Perfect for days when you'd like to eat bread.

Makes 4 open sandwiches

For the Crisp bread
2 cups (8 oz/225 g) almond meal (ground almonds) or equal quantities of linseeds, sunflower seeds and almonds, mixed and finely ground
1 cup basil leaves
½ cup (2½ oz/70 g) pumpkin seeds
1 tablespoon chia seeds
1 teaspoon cumin powder
¼ teaspoon chilli flakes
1 tablespoon filtered water
¼ teaspoon Himalayan pink salt or Celtic sea salt

For the Filling
1 avocado, peeled, seed removed and flesh mashed
1 cup (1 oz/30 g) mixed salad leaves
1 cup sprouts
1 tomato

For the Dressing
1 cup (3½ oz/100 g) mango, chopped
1 cup (3 oz/85 g) fresh coconut meat
¼ teaspoon chilli flakes
¼ teaspoon Himalayan pink salt or Celtic sea salt
¼ cup cilantro (coriander), roughly chopped

To make the crisp bread, place all the ingredients in the bowl of a blender and process until smooth. You may need to stop the machine and scrap down the ingredients from time to time, until it forms a dough-like texture.

On a sheet of Teflex or baking paper, press out the dough with your hands, cover the dough with another sheet of baking paper and roll a rolling pin over the top until smooth. Dehydrate for 2 hours, or bake at 50°C/120°F until crispy for 30 minutes.

To make the dressing, blend all the ingredients together in the bowl of a food processor.

Cut the crisp breads into 4 large squares. Spread each thickly with avocado, then top with mixed salad leaves, sprouts and tomato. Drizzle the dressing over.

Beetroot, Carrot and Pistachio Salad

Pistachios are high in vitamin B and are packed with essential nutrients. They're good for your heart too.

Serves 4

1 large beetroot (beet), peeled and washed
Filtered water, for soaking
¼ teaspoon Himalayan pink salt or Celtic sea salt
1 large carrot, peeled
2 cups (2 oz/60 g) mixed salad leaves

For the Pesto
¼ cup (1 oz/30 g) pistachio nuts
¼ cup (1 oz/30 g) pine nuts
1 teaspoon nutritional (savoury) yeast
½ cup fresh mint leaves, plus extra to garnish
¼ teaspoon chilli flakes
1 tablespoon chia seeds
¼ teaspoon Himalayan pink salt or Celtic sea salt
1 tablespoon olive oil

Using a vegetable spiraliser or vegetable peeler, thinly slice the beetroot so that it looks like pasta.

Soak the beetroot in filtered water with the salt for 5 minutes. Rinse and repeat 3 times or until the colour minimises.

Slice the carrot using the vegetable spiraliser. Place in a large bowl with the beetroot and mixed salad greens.

To make the pesto, reserve a few pistachio nuts then add the rest of the pistachios, the pine nuts, nutritional yeast, mint leaves, chilli flakes, chia seeds and salt to the bowl of a blender and blend until smooth. Drizzle the olive oil into the pesto and stir through by hand. Tip onto the salad and mix through until blended.

Garnish with fresh mint and the reserved pistachio nuts.

Kale and Basil Sauce for 'Pasta'

This sauce is perfect for drizzling over zucchini pasta, salads or pizzas.

Serves 2

2 cups (4½ oz/125 g) kale leaves, ribs removed, coarsely chopped
2 cup fresh basil leaves
1 garlic clove, coarsely chopped
¾ cup (3 oz/85 g) activated walnuts, coarsely chopped (see recipe)
¼ cup nutritional (savoury) yeast (optional)
¾ cup (6 fl oz/175 ml) extra virgin olive oil
Juice of 1 lemon
½ teaspoon Himalayan pink salt or Celtic sea salt
Freshly ground black pepper, to taste (optional)

Place all of the ingredients in a bowl of a food processor or blender. Process until the walnuts are small chunks.

Add more olive oil for a runnier sauce, if you like.

Zucchini Noodles with Satay Sauce

Enjoy this simple and satisfying meal anytime.

Serves 4

3 zucchini (courgettes)
1 large tomato
1 carrot
2 yellow squash
1 red capsicum (bell pepper)
1 Spanish (Bermuda) onion
½ cup (1½ oz/45 g) coconut flakes
½ cup (2 oz/60 g) pistachio nuts

For the Satay Sauce

3 teaspoons almond butter (see recipe)
Juice of 1 lime
2 teaspoons hemp seeds
2 teaspoons flaxseed oil
2 teaspoons apple cider vinegar
1 garlic clove

Use a spiraliser tool to make the zucchini into noodles and tip into a large bowl. Add the rest of the prepared vegetables, and combine with the noodles.

To make the satay sauce, blend the ingredients in the bowl of a blender or processor at high speed. Stir the satay sauce through the noodles until well combined.

Button Mushrooms

This simple Raw dish will wow your guests. It is easy to prepare and tastes even better the next day. You can add it to quinoa or salads, or eat it alongside a kale crisp bread and dip.

Serves 4

4 large button (white) mushrooms
¼ cup (2 fl oz/60 ml) olive oil
¼ cup (2 fl oz/60 ml) balsamic vinegar
1 tablespoon chia seeds
¼ teaspoon Himalayan pink salt or Celtic sea salt
¼ teaspoon cracked black pepper
Green salad leaves, to serve

Place the mushrooms in a large shallow bowl and pour over the oil and balsamic vinegar. Scatter chia seeds, salt and cracked black pepper over. Leave to marinate for 1–2 hours and serve with a garnish of green salad leaves.

Raw Pizza

Top this delicious pizza with sun-dried tomatoes and fresh basil leaves. It is also beautiful with a layer of avocado dip or Coriander Salsa Dip (*see recipes*) on the pizza crust.

Serves 4

For the Crust
1 cup (4 oz/115 g) LSA meal (mixed ground linseeds, sunflower seeds and almonds)
1 tablespoon dried oregano
1 tablespoon dried basil
1 tablespoon dried mixed herbs
2 cups (8 oz/225 g) yellow squash, chopped
1 cup (4 oz/115 g) walnuts, soaked for 1 hour in water
2 teaspoons Himalayan pink salt or Celtic sea salt
2 tablespoons olive oil
1 tablespoon lemon juice
½ shallot, chopped
2 teaspoons nutritional (savoury) yeast

For the Cashew Nut Cream
1 cup (4 oz/115 g) cashew nuts, soaked in filtered water for 1–2 hours
Juice of 1 lemon
¼ teaspoon Himalayan pink salt or Celtic sea salt
1 teaspoon maple syrup or Raw *honey*
1 tablespoon olive oil
¼ cup (2 fl oz/60 ml) filtered water

For the Tomato Sauce
1 cup (5 oz/150 g) tomatoes
1 cup (5 oz/150 g) sun-dried tomatoes, soaked in water for 20 minutes
¼ teaspoon dried basil
¼ teaspoon Himalayan pink salt or Celtic sea salt
1 teaspoon oregano

For the Macadamia Mozzarella Topping

1 cup (4 oz/115 g) macadamia nuts, soaked for 1 hour in water
¾ teaspoon lemon zest
1 tablespoon lemon juice
1 tablespoon chia seeds mixed with 1 cup (8 fl oz/250 ml) water
¼ shallot
¼ garlic clove
¼ teaspoon Himalayan pink salt or Celtic sea salt
¼ teaspoon cayenne pepper

To make the crust, mix the LSA meal, oregano, basil and mixed herbs in a bowl. Set aside.
Turn the dehydrator to 145°C/290°F. Process the remaining ingredients until smooth in the bowl of a blender or processor. Add the processed ingredients to the LSA and herb ingredients and stir well. Turn out onto a baking sheet lined with baking paper, press out to a ¼ in (0.5 cm) thick pizza base. Arrange on Teflex paper. Decrease the dehydrator temperature to 115°C/240°F and dehydrate for 45 minutes to 1 hour. Alternatively, bake in the oven for 30 minutes at 115°C/240°F.

To make the cashew nut cream, bend all the ingredients in the bowl of a food processor for 5 minutes, or until smooth and creamy.

To make the tomato sauce, blend all the ingredients in the bowl of a processor or blender until smooth and creamy.

To make the macadamia mozzarella topping, pulse all the ingredients in the bowl of a blender until the consistency of fine breadcrumbs.

Spread the cashew nut cream over the pizza crust then top tomato sauce and macadamia mozzarella.

Coconut and Rosemary Sweet Potato Chips

Sweet potatoes are very high in vitamins B6, C and D. They also contain magnesium, which helps to de-stress the body. These chips are an old favourite of mine. Serve as a snack or add to salads or the Raw food pizza and dips.

Serves 4

4 sweet potatoes
2 tablespoons coconut oil
2 sprigs fresh rosemary, leaves removed
¼ teaspoon Himalayan pink salt or Celtic sea salt

Cut the sweet potatoes into chips, place in a large ovenproof dish, drizzle over the coconut oil, rosemary and salt, stir well to thoroughly coat the potatoes.

Bake for 1 hour at 150°C/300°F, or until baked through.

Chickpea and Quinoa Patties with Salad

Quinoa is a supergrain, so-called because it contains 8 amino acids. Because of this it's considered a complete food. On its own it is a bland food, but takes on the flavour of other ingredients readily.

Makes 4–6 patties

1 cup (7 oz/200 g) quinoa, soaked overnight in filtered water, or use sprouted quinoa
2¼ cups (18 fl oz/550 ml) water
½ cup (2½ oz/75 g) pumpkin seeds
2 cups chickpeas, soaked overnight in filtered water
¼ cup sun-dried tomatoes
1 tablespoon tahini
2 tablespoons lemon juice
1 tablespoon cayenne pepper
¼ teaspoon Himalayan pink salt or Celtic sea salt
Black pepper, to taste
1 teaspoon garlic powder or 1 small garlic clove, crushed
2 tablespoons chives, snipped

For the Salad
1 cup (1 oz/30 g) spinach leaves
½ yellow capsicum (bell pepper), chopped
¼ Spanish (Bermuda) onion, diced
4 cherry tomatoes
¼ avocado, diced

For the Dressing
Olive oil
Juice of ½ lemon
¼ teaspoon cayenne pepper

To make the patties, rinse the sprouted quinoa and put in a pan with the water. Bring the water to the boil. Reduce to a simmer and let the quinoa cook until the water is absorbed and you can see some of the 'ribs' of the grain coming loose. Turn off the heat, fluff the quinoa, and let sit, covered, for 10 minutes.

Place the pumpkin seeds in a food processor and grind to a fine meal. Add the soaked chickpea and the quinoa and pulse to combine well.

Add the sun-dried tomatoes, tahini, lemon juice, cayenne pepper, salt, pepper, garlic and chives. Pulse continually until the mixture comes together. Add a little water, if necessary, until the mixture is easy to mould. Shape into patties and place on to Telflex or baking paper.

Dehydrate at 140°C/285°F for 4 hours, or bake at 115°C/240°F for 45 minutes, turning part way through the cooking.

To make the salad, in a large bowl, mix together the salad ingredients then divide between plates.

To make the dressing, put the ingredients in a glass jar, add a lid and shake vigorously.

Serve the patties with the salad and drizzle over the dressing.

Quinoa Burger with Hummus and Salad

Quinoa promotes energy production and the formation of healthy bones and teeth. Eat it regularly and reap the health rewards.

Serves 4

1 cup (7 oz/200 g) quinoa, sprouted (see introduction)
½ cup (2 oz/60 g) gluten-free flour such as quinoa, amaranth or millet
2 tablespoons coconut oil
1 teaspoon garlic powder
1 Spanish (Bermuda) onion, ground
1 cup (2 oz/60 g) spinach, finely chopped
1 cup (2¼ oz/65 g) kale, finely chopped
2 carrots, peeled and finely chopped
½ red capsicum (bell pepper), seeds removed and finely chopped
1 tablespoon cumin
½ teaspoon cayenne pepper
½ teaspoon mild curry powder
¼ teaspoon Himalayan pink salt or Celtic sea salt
½ teaspoon cracked pepper
Hummus, to serve (see recipe)
Mixed green salad, to serve
Lemon wedges, to serve

In a large bowl, mix the coconut oil with the garlic powder and onions. Add the spinach, kale, carrots and capsicum, then add the cumin, curry powder, salt and pepper. Mix in the quinoa, curry powder, salt and pepper and fold the mixture well.

Shape into burgers and line on Teflex paper, then dehydrate for 2–3 hours at 115°C/240°F, or line on baking paper and bake for 45 minutes at very low temperature.

Serve with green salad, a wedge of lemon and hummus.

Avocado and Kale Pesto with Zucchini Pasta

Zucchini is a great Raw food vegetable. It can be juiced, used in salads and spiralised to make pasta. It is a great anti-inflammatory food to eat.

Serves 4

4 medium zucchini (courgettes)
¼ teaspoon Himalayan pink salt or Celtic sea salt
¼ teaspoon cracked black pepper
3 garlic cloves
2 avocados
¼ cup (2 fl oz/60 ml) olive oil
¼ cup nutritional (savoury) yeast (optional)
½ cup (2 oz/60 g) pine nuts, plus a few extra to garnish
1 tablespoon lemon juice
¼ teaspoon chilli flakes
1 cup fresh basil
1 cup (2¼ oz/65 g) kale, stem discarded and leaves torn into small pieces
1 cup (6 oz/150 g) cherry tomatoes, halved
Mixed green salad, to serve

Spiralize the zucchini. Add to a colander to drain the excess liquid. Season with salt and pepper and set aside.

In the bowl of a food processor, blend the garlic with the avocados, olive oil, nutritional yeast, pine nuts, lemon juice, chilli flakes and half of the basil. Pulse until blended. Add the kale, and pulse until blended. Season to taste.

Tip into a large serving bowl, then stir through the zucchini and tomatoes. Serve with a fresh side salad of greens and the remaining basil.

Alfredo with Cashew Cream

This is a 'pasta'-style dish in which the zucchini replaces traditional pasta and the cashew nuts provide a creamy rich Italian taste. You almost think you are eating a rich dish but it is 100 per cent Raw gluten- free and nutritious.

Serves 4–6

2 zucchini (courgettes), sliced
6 cherry tomatoes, quartered or ¼ cup (1½ oz/45 g) sun-dried tomatoes
½ cup (2½ oz/75 g) black olives, chopped
1 tablespoon chia seeds
2 basil leaves, finely chopped
2 spring onions (scallions), finely chopped
⅓ cup (2½ fl oz/75 ml) olive oil
¼ teaspoon Himalayan pink salt or Celtic sea salt
¼ teaspoon cracked black pepper

For the Cashew Nut Cream
1 cup (4 oz/115 g) cashews, soaked for 1–2 hours in water
Juice of 1 lemon
1 teaspoon honey or maple syrup
¼ teaspoon Himalayan pink salt or Celtic sea salt
1 tablespoon olive oil
¼ cup (2 fl oz/60 ml) water

For the Macadamia Crumble
1 cup (4 oz/115 g) macadamia nuts, soaked for 1–2 hours
1 tablespoon almond milk
Pinch of salt

Spiralise the zucchini to make spaghetti. Add to a large bowl.

Make the cashew nut cream by blending all the ingredients together in the bowl of a food processor and then pulsing until combined. Mix the cashew nut cream through the zucchini.

To the bowl add the remaining salad ingredients Top with macadamia crumble (see recipe).

Chapter Seven

7 MAIN MEALS

Mint Falafel and Quinoa Couscous

Learning to add herbs and spices to your food makes the Raw food journey so much more tastier. Falafel are a fun 'fast food' but with the taste of a gourmet restaurant meal. The mint and lemon give this recipe a lovely clean and fresh, satisfying taste.

Makes 6

For the Falafel
2 tablespoons chia seeds
Juice of 1 lemon
1 cup (7 oz/200 g) chickpeas, canned and rinsed, or dried and soaked overnight in water
½ cup (3 oz/85 g) quinoa, cooked
1 cup (1 oz/30 g) spinach
1 cup mint, packed
½ cup basil, packed
½ cup fresh coriander (cilantro)
1 teaspoon cumin
1 teaspoon garlic powder
1 tablespoon olive oil
¼ teaspoon Himalayan pink salt or Celtic sea salt
¼ cup (1½ oz/45 g) quinoa flakes or quinoa flour, plus extra for dusting
1 teaspoon coconut oil
Iceberg lettuce, to serve
Cherry tomatoes, to serve
I tablespoon kefir yogurt, to serve

For the Quinoa Couscous

1 cup (8 fl oz/250 ml) boiling water
1 cup sprouted quinoa
1 tablespoon chia seeds
¼ teaspoon Himalayan pink salt or Celtic sea salt
1 tablespoon olive oil
1 garlic clove, sautéed in ½ teaspoon coconut oil
1 spring onion (scallion), finely chopped
½ cup (3 oz/85 g) sun-dried tomatoes
2 cups (12 oz/350 g) fresh tomatoes, finely chopped
1 cup basil

For the Dressing

2 tablespoons balsamic vinegar
Juice of 1 lemon
2 tablespoons olive oil
1 tablespoon chia seeds

To make the falafel, mix the chia seeds and lemon juice together in a bowl, and set aside to form a gel-like consistency for 5 minutes.

Process the chickpeas, quinoa, spinach, mint, basil, coriander, cumin, garlic, olive oil and salt. In the bowl of a food processor until it binds together. Take heaped dessertspoons of the mixture and roll into patties between the palms of your hand.

Dust the quinoa flakes or flour on a chopping board. Roll the falafel in the flakes to coat all around. In a pan, heat the coconut oil. Fry the falafel for 3–4 minutes on each side, or until golden brown. To make the couscous, pour the boiling water, couscous and chia seeds into a large bowl. Add the salt, and olive oil, stir, cover and set aside for 10 minutes.

Add the sautéed garlic, spring onion, sun-dried tomatoes, tomatoes and basil and stir to combine. To make the dressing, pour all the ingredients into a glass jar. Secure with a lid and shake well to combine. Season with salt and pepper to taste, then stir through the couscous.
Serve with iceburg lettuce, cherry tomatoes, and kefir yogurt.

Carrot and Activated Almond Salad

This vegan, gluten-free, grain-free and dairy-free Moroccan carrot salad is easy to make, sweet, and it's super nutritious too. It is perfect for a mid-week meal or a sociable gathering.

Serves 4

1 beetroot, sprialised or grated (shredded)
Himalayan pink salt
3 large carrots, spiralised with a spiraliser or peeler
½ cup (2 oz/60 g) mixed activated sliced almonds, (skinless), pumpkin and chia seeds
2 tablespoons raisins
1 Spanish (Bermuda) onion, halved and sliced
1 red capsicum (bell pepper), thinly sliced
1 cup fresh coriander (cilantro), chopped
1 cup fresh flat leaf parsley, to serve
⅓ cup mint leaves, chopped, to garnish

For the Dressing
2 tablespoons extra virgin olive oil
Juice and zest of 1 lemon
1 tablespoon chia seeds
1 teaspoon maple syrup
1 teaspoon ground cinnamon
½ teaspoon ground cumin
Himalayan pink salt or Celtic sea salt and cracked black pepper, to taste
1 teaspoon fresh root ginger, grated (shredded)
¼ teaspoon chilli flakes

Put the beetroot in a bowl of filtered water with ½ teaspoon salt. Set aside.

Put the spiralised carrots in a large bowl and mix in the remaining salad ingredients including the soaked and drained beetroot.

To make the dressing, mix all the ingredients in a small jar, secure the lid and shake well to combine. Mix the dressing thoroughly through the salad.

Serve on top of a bed of flat-leaf parsley and scatter mint leaves on top.

Thai Cashew Curried Salad with Coconut Meat

Coconut meat is becoming a popular ingredient in the Raw food lifestyle. Coconut meat is known to kill disease causing bacteria, fungi, yeast and viruses because of the anti-microbial effects of the fatty acids. There are many other health benefits that include helping protect against heart disease.

Serves 4

4 cups mixed salad
½ cup (3 oz/85 g) sun-dried tomatoes, finely chopped
1 avocado, sliced
½ red capsicum (bell pepper)
½ yellow capsicum (bell pepper)
½ green capsicum (bell pepper)
Himalayan pink salt or Celtic sea salt, to taste
Cracked black pepper
1 tablespoon coconut meat, finely chopped
1 tablespoon chia seeds, to taste
1 shallot, finely chopped
½ cup continental parsley
½ cup Spicy Cashews (see recipe below)
½ cup Thai Dressing (see recipe below)

For the Thai Dressing
½ cup (4 fl oz/125 ml) sesame oil
½ cup (4 fl oz/125 ml) gluten-free tamari soy sauce
½ cup (4 fl oz/125 ml) olive oil
½ cup (4 fl oz/125 ml) lime juice
1 tablespoon maple syrup
2 Thai chilies or 1½ teaspoons chilli flakes
¼ teaspoon Himalayan pink salt or Celtic sea salt
¼ cup (2 oz/60 g) cashew nuts

For the Spicy Cashews

2 cups (8 oz/225 g) cashew nuts, soaked in water for 1–2 hours
1 tablespoon honey
2 tablespoons maple syrup
1 teaspoon turmeric
¼ teaspoon chilli flakes
¼ teaspoon Himalayan pink salt or Celtic sea salt

Place the mixed salad in a large, shallow salad bowl, top with sun-dried tomatoes, avocado, bell peppers, shallots and parsley and season with a generous amount of salt and pepper. Top with coconut meat.

To make the Thai dressing, blend all the ingredients together in the bowl of a food processor or blender on low speed until smooth. Tip over the salad.

To make the spicy cashews, place the nut in a bowl, drizzle over the honey and maple syrup and stir well to coat. Add the turmeric, chilli flakes and salt. Mix until well coated.

Dehydrate for 1 hour at 115°C/240°F, or bake at 85°C/185°F heat for 10–15 minutes. Tip over the salad.

Pad Thai

Here is my version or a Raw pad Thai. The zucchini replaces the noodles and the coconut lime dressing giving it a lovely zest and Thai taste. Bell peppers are high in Vitamin C; they contain fibre, protein and iron. I love the colours created in this dish.

Serves 4

2 zucchini (courgettes), spiralised
1 carrot, spiralised
2 cups (1 lb/450 g) beansprouts
1 yellow capsicum (bell pepper), sliced
4 spring onions (scallions), diced
¾ cup (3 oz/85 g) cashews, chopped
½ cup fresh coriander (cilantro), chopped
Juice of 1 lime
1 tablespoon olive oil
¼ teaspoon Himalayan pink salt or Celtic sea salt
⅓ cup mint leaves, to garnish

For the Coconut and Lime Dressing
1 garlic clove, crushed
1 tablespoon fresh turmeric, grated (shredded)
½ tablespoon fresh root ginger, grated (shredded)
Juice of 4 limes
1 teaspoon manuka honey or alternative sweetener such as stevia or palm sugar
2 tablespoons coconut kefir or coconut milk

To make the dressing, blend all the ingredients until smooth in the bowl of a food processor or blender.

To make the pad Thai, tip all the ingredients into a large bowl, season to taste, then add the beansprouts, peppers, spring onion and cashew nuts.

Stir the dressing through the vegetables. Garnish with fresh mint leaves.

Raw Italian Pasta

This recipe may look complicated but really it's simple. I love using cayenne pepper in my diet because of its health benefits, especially for the heart. Cayenne pepper removes the plaque adhering to the arteries.

For the Pasta
1 zucchini (courgette), per person

For the Tomato Sauce
½ cup (3 oz/85 g) semi-dried tomatoes
¼ cup (1 oz/30 g) activated almonds, skins removed
½ teaspoon chilli flakes
1 tablespoon balsamic vinegar
½ cup (4 fl oz/125 ml) extra virgin olive oil
Himalayan pink salt or Celtic sea salt, to taste

For the Beet Balls
1 cup Raw beetroot (beet), grated (shredded)
½ carrot, grated (shredded)
1 cup (4 oz/115 g) Activated Walnuts (see Nuts chapter)
1 tablespoon tahini
¼ teaspoon cayenne pepper
½ teaspoon garlic
¼ teaspoon Himalayan pink salt or Celtic sea salt
1 teaspoon olive oil
¼ cup chopped parsley
1 teaspoon chia seeds

For the Raw Pesto
1 cup (4 oz/115 g) cashew nuts, pine nuts or macadamia nuts
1 cup fresh basil
1 garlic clove, crushed
Himalayan pink salt or Celtic sea salt
1 tablespoon extra virgin olive oil

To make the pasta, use a spiraliser to make noodles from the zucchini. Set aside in a large mixing bowl.

To make the tomato sauce, process all the ingredients in the bowl of a food processor or blender, until smooth.

Toss the zucchini noodles together with the tomato sauce.

To make the beet balls, combine all the ingredients in a large bowl. Take a dessertspoon-sized amount and roll into balls between the palms of your hands.

To make the pesto, process all the ingredients in the bowl of a food processor or blender at low speed until smooth.

Serve the beet balls on top of **Raw** pasta with pesto and tomato sauce. Serve with a wedge of orange, fresh parsley or mint to remove garlic odour from the breath.

Chapter Eight

SNACKS

8

Sauerkraut

The lactic acid process that naturally preserves sauerkraut is ripe with probiotic power. The good bacteria that are common to preserved food include *Lactobacillus acidophilus*, *L. bulgaricus*, *L. plantarum*, *L. caret*, *L. pentoaceticus*, *L. brevis* and *L. thermophiles*. There is a wide range of healthy bacteria responsible for these tasty ferments, so you won't find the same good bacteria count in every batch, but what you will find is a product brimming with healthy probiotics that will help ensure good gut health.

1 red cabbage
2 carrots
2 tablespoons Himalayan pink salt
1 teaspoon celery seeds
1 teaspoon dill seeds, divided
1 teaspoon black peppercorns, divided
1 bay leaf

Shred, slice or grate the cabbage and carrots and place in a large bowl.

Add the salt and toss to combine, then set aside for 30 minutes.

Knead the vegetables by pressing them down with your hands. Tip them into a mason jar, add the spices or any other spices you like and press down on the vegetables. Water will leach from the vegetables, then over time it will subside.

If there is no water you can make a brine, to help cover the vegetables. To make the brine, bring ½ cup water and a ½ teaspoon Himalayan salt to the boil and stir until the salt dissolves, then leave to cool. Pour over the vegetables, leaving 1 in (2.5 cm) of head space in each jar. Add a weight to help press the vegetables down Seal the jars. You will see them bubbling over the next few days.

Once a day loosen the lid to let the fermentation gases escape. Push any vegetables that have worked their way up the side of the jar or around the weight back down into the liquid.

As the lactic acid bacteria proliferates, the cabbage will turn into sauerkraut. Theoretically the cabbage is ALIVE with probiotics, and by day 4 it can be eaten. However, for best flavour leave it for 1–3 weeks. Warmer climates speed up fermentation, while cooler temperatures slow the process. Refrigerating slows down the process so once ready store in the refrigerator.

Apple Bars

This is lovely Raw, sweet and satisfying apple bar that you can enjoy as a light snack between meals or to give you energy while you're on the go. It'll keep energy stores full and sugar cravings at bay.

Makes 3 or 4 bars

1 cup (4 oz/115 g) LSA or almond meal (ground almonds)
1 green apple, peeled and chopped
1 cup fresh dates, packed
¼ cup (1¼ oz/35 g) pumpkin seeds
2 teaspoon ground cinnamon
2 tablespoons chia seeds

Process all the ingredients in the bowl of a food processor or blender until it binds together. Tip into a lined baking tray and press out to 1 in (2.5 cm) thick.

Dehydrate for 3–4 hours at 115°C/240°F, or lightly bake in an oven set to 70°C/160°F for 1 hour. to dry out. Alternatively set in the refrigerator for up to 7 days. Slice into bars and eat Raw.

Lucia's Raw Cinnamon Bars

Apple and cinnamon are a match made in heaven and healthy too.

Serves 1–2

1 apple, peeled and finely chopped
½ cup (2½ oz/75 g) cranberries
½ cup (2 oz/60 g) almonds
1 teaspoon ground cinnamon powder
1 teaspoon pumpkin seeds, to decorate

Process all the ingredients until coarse, mould into a bar, decorate with pumpkin seeds and set on baking paper or silicone sheets. Dehydrate for 4–6 hours.

Ginger Goji Chia Crunch

Enjoy as a mid-afternoon healthy snack or natural sugar fix. This snack is great for those who have a sugar craving and are trying to change old habits. It's very satisfying too. Enjoy with peppermint tea.

Serves 1–2

1 cup (5 oz/140 g) pumpkin seeds
½ cup (2½ oz/75 g) sunflower seeds
1 tablespoon chia seeds
½ cup (2 oz/60 g) goji berries
1 teaspoon cacao powder
½ teaspoon ginger spice
1 teaspoon coconut oil

Mix the cacao powder and coconut oil together in a small bowl. Put all the other ingredients in a large mixing bowl, mix well, then stir the contents of the small bowl into the larger one. Add some fresh strawberries, if you like. If you want the chocolate to set, then place into the refrigerator for 5 minutes.

Marinated Olives

Olives are healing to the body and are especially good for the digestive system. They are a great source of iron. Black olives are rich in fatty acids and anti-oxidants that nourish, hydrate and protect.

3 cups (1 lb 2 oz/500 g) Kalamata olives, pits removed
½ teaspoon ground coriander
¼ cup mint leaves, chopped
¼ cup parsley, chopped
¼ cup (2 fl oz/60 ml) olive oil
1 tablespoon lime zest
¼ teaspoon Himalayan pink salt or Celtic sea salt

Goji Cacao Maca Bars

Maca powder is an ancient root, that belongs to the radish family. It is rich in vitamins B, C and E, and high in calcium, zinc, iron, magnesium, phosphorous and amino acids. You can add it to your smoothies, salads, drinks and juices but I enjoy adding it to these goji cacao maca bars,

Makes 6–8

2 cups (8 oz/225 g) almonds, ground to crumbs
2 cups (8 oz/225 g) cashew nut pieces
1 cup (5 oz/150 g) hemp seeds
½ cup (2½ oz/75 g) flax seeds, soaked for at least 2 hours and drained
¼ teaspoon Himalayan pink salt or Celtic sea salt
1 teaspoon vanilla extract
1 teaspoon lemon zest, finely chopped
1 cup (8 oz/225 g) maple syrup or honey
¼ cup maca powder
¼ cup cacao nibs
1 cup (4 oz/115 g) goji berries, soaked in water for 10 minutes, then drained

For the Cacao Sauce
1½ cups cacao nibs
1 cup (8 oz/225 g) maple syrup or ½ cup stevia
½ cup (4 fl oz/125 ml) coconut oil

Mix all the ingredients in a large bowl until well combined. Spread evenly on baking paper or Teflex sheets to a rectangle 8–12 in (20–30 cm) wide x 4 in (10 cm) long. Dehydrate overnight or set in the refrigerator.

On a chopping board, cut into bars with a pizza cutter. Glaze with cacao sauce.

To make the cacao sauce, blend all the ingredients in the bowl of a food processor or blender until smooth. Store in a squeeze bottle in the refrigerator.

Blueberry Granola Bar

A great snack to help keep energy levels raised and cravings at bay. These bars are packed with nuts, seeds and blueberries and have a hint of lemon and sweetness.

Makes 50 bars

6 cups (1 lb 14 oz/850 g) frozen blueberries
2 cups (8 oz/225 g) almonds, finely ground
1 cup (4 oz/115 g) cashew nut pieces, ground to nibs
1 cup (4 oz/115 g) walnut pieces
½ cup (2½ oz/75 g) sunflower seeds
1 tablespoon chia seeds
¼ cup (2½ oz/75 g) flax seeds, soaked in filtered water for 2 hours, then drained
½ cup (4 fl oz/125 ml) maple syrup
2 teaspoons almond extract
1 teaspoon lemon zest, finely chopped
¼ teaspoon Himalayan pink salt or Celtic sea salt

Line the tray of a dehydrator with baking paper or Teflex sheets. Pour half the blueberries onto the baking paper, then place another sheet of baking paper on the tray beneath to catch any liquid. Dehydrate at 115°F/240°F for 8 hours.

In a large bowl, mix the dehydrated blueberries with the remaining ingredients until they are evenly mixed. Spread the mixture evenly on lined sheets of a dehydrator tray. Dehydrate overnight at 115°C/240°F.

Slice into bars (30 per sheet). Return to the dehydrator for another 8 hours.

Chocolate Ginger Chia Macaroons

Looking for a healthy snack alternative? These bars are the perfect mid-afternoon pick me up.

Makes 20

1 cup (3 oz/85 g) desiccated (dry unsweetened shredded) coconut
1 cup (4 oz/115 g) macadamia nuts
¾ cup (3 oz/85 g) cacao powder
½ cup (2 fl oz/60 ml) maple syrup
1 fresh date
1 tablespoon coconut oil
1 tablespoon ground ginger
1 teaspoon vanilla extract
Himalayan pink salt or Celtic sea salt, to taste

Blend all ingredients well in the bowl of a food processor or blender.

Roll and shape into small balls. Store in the freezer or refrigerator and take out 5 minutes before serving.

Serve with a green tea or soy milk chai latte and fresh strawberries.

Chocolates Truffles

Living a **Raw** Food lifestyle doesn't mean you have to miss out on having a treat from time to time. It's all about keeping everything in balance. Aim for 80 per cent **Raw** and 20 per cent cooked food. Keep sugar to a minimum and when you feel like a treat you can whip up this amazing recipe.

Makes 22–24

½ cup (2 oz/60 g) almonds
½ cup (2 oz/60 g) (mixed ground linseeds, sunflower seeds and almonds)
6 fresh dates
1 tablespoon coconut oil
1 tablespoon chia seeds
1 tablespoon maple syrup
3 tablespoons cacao powder
Desiccated (dry, unsweetened, shredded) coconut, for coating

Blend all the ingredients except for the coconut in the bowl of a food processor or blender until smooth. Roll into small balls. Coat with coconut and freeze on baking trays.

Chocolate Ginger Macaroons

These macaroons are easy to make and great to keep stored in the freezer for those days when you need a quick fix, or something to provide a boost of energy. The ginger flavour works well with the Raw cacao powder to add intense flavour without the need for too much sweetener.

Makes 22–24

1 tablespoon chia seeds
1 cup (3 oz/85 g) desiccated (dry, unsweetened, shredded) coconut
1 cup (4 oz/115 g) macadamia nuts
¾ cup (3 oz/85 g) cacao powder
½ cup (2 fl oz/60 ml) maple syrup
1 fresh date
1 tablespoon coconut oil
1 tablespoon ground ginger
1 teaspoon vanilla extract
¼ teaspoon Himalayan pink salt or Celtic sea salt

Blend all the ingredients in the bowl of a food processor or blender until it binds together. Roll and shape into small balls.

Store in the freezer or refrigerator and take out 5 minutes before serving.

Raspberry Jam

The taste of this jam is intense and will provide a sustained release of energy.

1 cup (5 oz/150 g) frozen raspberries
⅓ cup (2 oz/55 g) chia seeds

Allow the frozen berries to thaw. Blend all ingredients in a food processor until smooth. Store in a glass jar in the refrigerator for up to 7 days.

Strawberry Jam

Enjoy with sourdough, pancakes or coconut kefir yogurt.

1 cup (4 oz/115 g) fresh strawberries
1 tablespoon maple syrup
⅓ cup (2 oz/60 g) chia seeds

Blend all the ingredients in a food processor until smooth. Store in a glass jar in the refrigerator for up to 7 days.

Chocolate Balls

Living a Raw food lifestyle doesn't mean that you have to go without your favourite foods. Keep these for an occasional indulgence.

1 cup (4 oz/115 g) almonds
2 tablespoons cacao powder, plus 1 tablespoon for dusting
1 tablespoon coconut oil
3 fresh dates
1 tablespoon filtered water

Blend all the ingredients in the bowl of a food processor until well blended. Take a teaspoon of the mixture and roll into little balls. Place the cacao in a bowl and roll the balls in the cacao.

Store in the freezer and thaw before eating. Serve with strawberries or green tea.

Chocolate Chia Sauce

Use this sweet jam on gluten-free sourdoughs with a spoonful of coconut kefir and you'll think you're eating scones, jam and cream; this version is nutrient-rich to provide you with energy.

2 teaspoons chia seeds
1 tablespoon cacao powder
¼ cup (2 fl oz/60 ml) maple syrup
1 teaspoon vanilla extract

Stir all ingredients well. Store covered in a glass container in the refrigerator for up to 5 days.

Chapter Nine
9 DESSERTS

Peach Cream Chocolate Cake

This is a very creamy, rich and smooth Raw food dessert that's great to serve when entertaining friends. Keep it in the freezer or refrigerate if for up to 7 days – if it lasts that long! Pouring the chocolate sauce on top and keeping it smooth can be tricky so make sure your base and filling is frozen before you pour on the top layer.

Serves 8–10

For the Chocolate Crust
½ cup (4 fl oz/125 ml) coconut oil
¼ cup (2 oz/60 g) cacao powder
2 teaspoons honey
2 teaspoons cacao butter, melted

For the Peach Cream
1½ cups (6 oz/175 g) macadamia nuts
1 peach, plus 1 extra peach, to decorate
1 banana
1 teaspoon vanilla extract
1 teaspoon honey
2 teaspoons coconut oil, plus extra for greasing

For the Chocolate Sauce Topping
2 tablespoons coconut oil
3 tablespoons unsweetened cacoa powder
1 tablespoon maple syrup
¼ teaspoon Himalayan pink salt or Celtic sea salt

To make the chocolate crust, tip all the ingredients into the bowl of a food processor or blender and process until smooth. Tip into a 10 in (25 cm) flan dish lightly greased with coconut oil and press out to the sides. Put in the freezer to set.

To make the peach cream, process all the ingredients in the bowl of a blender or food processor until smooth. Pour over the crust. Put in the freezer.

To make the chocolate sauce topping, blend the ingredients in the bowl of a food processor, and tip over the peach filling.

Slice the remaining peach finely and arrange on the cream.

Store in the freezer and bring out 5 minutes before serving. Store in the refrigerator or freezer for up to 7 days.

Kiwi and Lime Cheesecake

You can substitute pitted dates for fresh in this recipe, and soak them for an hour to soften and use as a sweetener instead of honey. The less sugar you have in your body the less you will crave sweet things.

Serves 6–8

For the Crust

1 cup (3 oz/85 g) desiccated (dry, unsweetened, shredded) coconut
1 tablespoon chia seeds
½ cup (2 oz/60 g) linseed meal (ground linseeds)
½ cup quinoa flakes
Himalayan pink salt or Celtic sea salt, to taste
2 fresh dates
1 tablespoon coconut oil, plus extra for greasing

For the Filling

1 cup (4 oz/115 g) cashew nuts, soaked in filtered water for 1 hour
1 cup (4 oz/115 g) macadamia nuts, soaked in filtered water for 1 hour
1 cup (8 fl oz/250 ml) lime juice
1 tablespoon honey
1 teaspoon vanilla extract
3 tablespoons coconut oil, melted
Zest of 1 lime
1 tablespoon chia seeds
3 kiwi fruit, sliced, to decorate

To make the crust, mix all the ingredients together in a large bowl, tip into a 25 cm (10 in) non-stick flan dish, greased with a little coconut oil, and press out to the edges and up the sides, flattening as you go with the back of a spoon. Place in the freezer to set.

To make the filling, blend all the ingredients in the bowl of a food processor until smooth. Smooth out on top of the crust.

Top with sliced kiwi fruit. Serve cold.

Chocolate Cheesecake

Did you know that Raw cacao benefits human longevity and health without negative side effects? You can eat your chocolate treats and enjoy positive health benefits on the Raw food lifestyle. There's no guilt with this dessert, and it tastes divine.

Serves 8

For the Crust
1 cup (4 oz/115 g) almonds
½ cup (4 fl oz/125 ml) coconut oil, warmed to liquid, plus extra for greasing
3 fresh dates (use ½ cup pitted dates, soaked, if you can't get fresh)
1 tablespoon honey or maple syrup
¼ teaspoon Himalayan pink salt or Celtic sea salt

For the Filling
1 cup (4 oz/115 g) cashew nuts, soaked in filtered water for 3 hours
1 banana, frozen
½ avocado
⅓ cup (2 ½ fl oz/75 ml) maple syrup
½ cup (4 oz/115 g) cacao powder
½ cup (4 fl oz/125 ml) coconut oil, warmed to liquid
1 teaspoon vanilla extract

To make the crust, blend all the ingredients in the bowl of a food processor or blender until it binds together. Press out into a 25 cm (10 in) flan dish, lightly greased with coconut oil, and press up the sides. Freeze to set.

To make the filling, blend all the ingredients in the bowl of a processor or blender and spread onto the crust. Transfer the dish to the freezer, until set. Remove 5–10 minutes before serving.

Coconut and Lime Cheesecake

If you love citrus flavours then you'll love this indulgence.

Serves 6–8

For the Crust
1 cup (4 oz/115 g) almond meal (ground almonds)
¾ cup medjool dates

For the Filling
2 medium avocados
1 tablespoon honey or maple syrup
½ cup (4 fl oz/125 ml) lime juice
5 tablespoons coconut oil, melted, plus extra for greasing
½ cup (1½ oz/45 g) desiccated (dry, unsweetened, shredded) coconut

To make the crust, blend or process the almond meal with the medjool dates. Tip into a 25 cm
(10 in) greased flan dish and use the back of a spoon to press the crust out to the edges, flattening as
you go.

To make the filling, blend all the ingredients, until smooth, in the bowl of a food processor or blender
and spread on top of the crust. Transfer the flan dish to the freezer, until set. Remove 5–10 minutes
before serving.

Chocolate Beetroot Tart

This lovely Raw dessert is moist and very satisfying. The beetroot contains a detoxifying element, and contains a powerful dose of anti-oxidants.

Serves 8

For the Crust
½ cup (4 fl oz/250 ml) coconut oil, melted
1 cup (4 oz/115 g) cacao powder
½ cup (2 oz/60 g) quinoa flour
½ cup (2 oz/60 g) flax meal
2 tablespoons chia seeds
1 cup (8 fl oz/250 ml) honey or maple syrup
1 cup (4 oz/115 g) cashew nuts, processed
Himalayan pink salt or Celtic sea salt, to taste

For the Filling
1 beetroot (beet), chopped
½ cup (2 oz/60 g) cashew nuts, soaked for 2 hours in filtered water
½ cup (2 fl oz/60 ml) filtered water
3 tablespoons coconut oil, melted, plus extra for greasing
½ cup (2 oz/60 g) cacao powder
1 tablespoon honey or maple syrup
2 fresh dates
¼ teaspoon Himalayan pink salt or Celtic sea salt
Fresh strawberries, to serve

To make the crust, mix the coconut oil in a bowl with the cacao, quinoa flour, flax meal, chia seeds, honey, cashew nuts and salt. Tip into a greased 10 in (25 cm) round dish and spread out to the edges, flattening the mixture as you go, with the back of a spoon. Chill in the freezer.

To make the filling, blend all the ingredients in the bowl of a food processor or blender until very smooth. Pour into the crust and freeze overnight. Serve sliced on its own or with fresh strawberries. Keeps well in the freezer in plastic wrap (cling film).

Banoffee Pie

This is my absolute favourite dessert to make. It tastes great topped with fresh bananas and the coconut yogurt adds a creamy texture. This one will wow your guests.

Serves 6–8

For the Crust
1 cup (4 oz/115 g) almonds
3 fresh dates (use ½ cup pitted dates, soaked, if you can't get fresh)
1 tablespoon honey or maple syrup

For the Filling
2 tablespoons coconut oil, plus extra for greasing
3 tablespoons cacao powder
2 tablespoons honey
¼ teaspoon Himalayan pink salt or Celtic sea salt

For the Topping
1 cup (4 oz/115 g) soaked cashew nuts
¼ cup fresh coconut
⅓ cup (2½ fl oz/75 ml) filtered water
Juice of 2 lemons
Zest of 1 lemon
2 bananas, sliced, to decorate

To make the crust, blend all the ingredients in the bowl of a food processor or blender until it binds together. Press out into a 10 in (25 cm) flan dish lightly greased with coconut oil, and press up the sides. Freeze to set.

To make the filling, melt the coconut oil, then stir in the cacao powder, honey and salt. Pour the filling on top of the crust, then freeze again until set.

Blend all the topping ingredients in a food processor until smooth and creamy. Spread on top of the filling with sliced bananas.

Raw Strawberry Chocolate Trifle

This dessert is very rich so it's perfect to serve in small slices.

Serves 6

10½ oz (290 g) strawberries, sliced

For the Crunchy Base Layer
½ cup (2 oz/60 g) pecans
2 dates, coarsely chopped

For the Ganache Layer
⅓ cup (2½ fl oz/75 ml) coconut oil, melted
⅓ cup (2½ fl oz/75 ml) maple syrup or alternative liquid sweetener
⅓ cup (1¼ oz/635 g) cacao powder

For the Chocolate 'Mousse'
½ avocado
1 tablespoon cacao powder
1 tablespoon maple syrup

For the Vanilla 'Mousse'
1 cup (4 oz/115 g) cashews, soaked in filtered water for 2 hours until soft
⅓ cup (2½ fl oz/75 ml) maple syrup
⅓ cup (2½ fl oz/75 ml) filtered water
⅓ cup (2½ fl oz/75 ml) coconut oil, melted
Seeds from 1 vanilla bean (pod) or 1 teaspoon vanilla extract

To make the base, blend the pecans and dates in the bowl of a food processor or blender until well combined.

To make the ganache, whisk all the ingredients together in a bowl until smooth and well combined.

To make the chocolate mousse, add all the ingredients to a bowl, and mix until smooth and mousse-like. Refrigerate until set.

To make the vanilla mousse, place all the ingredients in the bowl of a blender and blend until smooth. Refrigerate until set.

To assemble the trifle, use a large glass bowl or several smaller ones. Layer the crunchy base layer, ganache, chocolate mousse, sliced strawberries and vanilla"mousse, in layers.

Chia Freekeh Pudding

This dessert is perfect for those who love the taste of cinnamon. You could even eat it for breakfast, since the main ingredient, freekeh, is a young green grain, known for its high nutritional content.

Serves 4

½ cup (2½ oz/75 g) chia seeds
2 cups (16 fl oz/500 ml) Almond Milk (see recipe)
1 cup sprouted freekeh (see introduction)
½ cup medjool dates, chopped, seeds removed
2 teaspoons ground cinnamon powder
2 tablespoons cranberries
¼ cup (2 fl oz/60 ml) maple syrup

Soak the chia seeds in the almond milk in a bowl for 5 minutes.

Add the sprouted quinoa, almond milk and chia seeds, dates, cinnamon, cranberries and maple syrup to a large bowl and stir well.

Ice Cream Cones

Serve this delicious treat with camomile or peppermint tea.

Serves 6

For the Cones
1¼ cups (5 oz/150 g) flax meal
¾ cup pear or peach, chopped
½ cup (1½ oz/45 g) young coconut meat
2 teaspoons lemon juice
1¼ cups (½ pint/300 ml) water
⅓ cup (2½ fl oz/75 ml) maple syrup
¼ teaspoon Himalayan pink salt or Celtic sea salt
¾ teaspoon vanilla extract

For the Chocolate Ice Cream
4 bananas, frozen
½ cup (2 oz/60 g) cacao powder
⅓ cup (2½ fl oz/75 ml) maple syrup
¼ teaspoon Himalayan pink salt or Celtic sea salt
4 fresh dates
Cacao nibs, to decorate

To make the cones, add all the ingredients to a large bowl. Mix thoroughly. Spread a thin layer on Teflex or baking paper and place on a baking tray. Freeze until firm. The mixture will set to be very pliable. You can mould it into cones.

To make the chocolate ice cream, put the frozen bananas, cacao, maple syrup and salt in the bowl of a blender. Start on low speed and steadily increase to high speed to blend. Add the dates and pulse a few times, just enough to break them into small pieces, then continue to blend for 5 minutes, or until smooth. Top with cacao nibs.

Lucia's Apple Pudding

Apple and cinnamon are a taste combination made in heaven.

Serves 4

2 green apples
1 tablespoon ground cinnamon powder

For the Base
1 cup (4 oz/115 g) walnuts
¼ cup desiccated (dry, unsweetened, shredded) coconut
¼ cup fresh dates
1 tablespoon coconut oil
1 tablespoon honey
1 tablespoon ground cinnamon powder

For the Apple Filling
1 green apple
2 bananas
½ cup (2½ oz/75 g) chia seeds
Juice of 1 lemon
1 tablespoon maple syrup

To make the base, blend the walnuts coarsely in the bowl of a food processor or blender. Add the rest of the ingredients and blend until a dough-like consistency. Spoon the mixture into a 10 in (25 cm) flan dish and spread evenly over the base, flattening as you go.

To make the filling, blend 1 apple with the bananas, chia seeds, lemon juice and maple syrup. Set aside for 10 minutes to form a glutinous texture.

Slice the remaining apples and arrange half over the crust. Dust with the cinnamon. Spoon the filling on top, then top with the apples.

Dehydrate for 1 hour, or bake in the oven at 115°C/240°F for 1 hour and 15 minutes.

Raw Goji Berry Chocolate Cake

Do you crave chocolate? Cacao powder is full of nutrients. It looks like cocoa but retains all its natural goodness making it a good substitute to eat when you crave chocolate.

Serves 4

1 cup (8 fl oz/250 ml) coconut oil
1 cup (8 oz/225 g) Raw cacao powder
½ cup (2½ oz/75 g) goji berries, plus extra to decorate
½ cup (2½ oz/75 g) cranberries, plus extra to decorate
½ teaspoon Himalayan sea salt

Melt the coconut oil in a pan over gentle heat until liquid. Add the cacao powder and salt and stir through. Add the goji berries and cranberries. Pour into a 6½ x 4 in (17 x 11 cm) container lined with baking paper. Add more berries pushing them into the top for decoration.

Chocolate Chia Pudding

This is a quick sweet fix, but healthy and light. The chia seeds swell up and make a lovely soft texture with a gentle chocolate taste. If you haven't got blueberries you could try adding goji berries as they soften well in this recipe and taste great with the chia pudding.

Serves 1

2 tablespoons chia seeds
½ cup (4 fl oz/125 ml) coconut water
1 tablespoon cacao powder
1 teaspoon cacao nibs
1 teaspoon maple syrup or honey
1 teaspoon Almond Butter (see recipe)
½ cup (2 oz/60 g) blueberries

Combine the chia seeds with the coconut water in a bowl and stir well. Set aside for 10 minutes, stirring frequently.

Add the rest of the ingredients to the bowl and then set aside until thickened, 10 minutes.

Goji Berry Chia Seed Pudding

This is a quick and lovely dessert or snack made with homemade almond milk. Easily digested, it offers a great way to change old habits from eating processed chocolate or packaged sweets. This will store well in the refrigerator overnight and the flavours are better the next day

Serves 1

1 cup Almond Milk (see recipe)
2 tablespoons chia seeds
1 teaspoon cinnamon powder
1 tablespoon goji berries
1 tablespoon cacao nibs

Mix the almond milk, chia seeds, cinnamon, goji berries and cacao nibs together in a bowl. Stir well and allow to set for 10 minutes, or set in the refrigerator overnight.

Serve on its own as a dessert or treat, or top with fresh strawberries and drizzle **Raw** honey on top for extra sweetness.

In closing...

'Live your life with passion' is my motto. Eat clean food, think positively and love and appreciate nature for providing such an abundance of healthy food.

I used to cook very bland food, always using the same trusty old recipes. Since stepping outside my comfort zone and embracing a more creative style of eating, I've come to enjoy and appreciate natural food and its awesome healing power. Nature provides fresh, living foods such as fruit, vegetables, nuts and seeds, to be enjoyed as they are, without interference from cooking or the addition of artificial additives. Creating *Cooking with Chia* and *The Power of Living Raw* has taken me on a wonderful journey, which has increased my awareness and knowledge of food. I always considered myself a healthy eater, but as soon as I began the live/**Raw** food lifestyle I have gained energy, increased creativity and feel a sense of calm and inner peace around food. When we eat processed foods that are high in sugar or gluten, or we eat over-cooked foods, or too much meat, the body is thrown out of balance, creating sugar cravings, chronic fatigue, digestive disorders and even eating disorders... all of which I have experienced. Now I've changed my way of eating I'm able to maintain a healthy body weight without ever feeling like I'm on a diet. Looking after your body is vital for longevity and happiness. Most people think they need to eat more than they actually do. The digestive system copes better with less and especially food that is gluten-free, diary-free and sugar-free. Eating a wide variety of wholesome, seasonal foods in many different colours will ensure you are getting a varied diet. Every natural and living **Raw** food has healthy qualities and healing benefits.

Learning to look after your digestive system, balance your hormones, and rejuvenate your body and mind is a 21st-century philosophy for living. It is not a diet, it is a way of life. The magic of nature is inescapable. My girls and I say a gratitude prayer before every meal in appreciation of the energizing meal we're about to enjoy.

Nicky

For more information about yoga and **Raw** food retreats, email nicky@nickyarthur.com
Instagram: nickyarthur2
FB **Raw** by Nicky Arthur
Twitter
www.nickyarthur.com

Index

With thanks...

Thank you to Suzie Cheetham who has been a big help. You came into my life at the right time.

To my dream team in the week of the photoshoot and for your friendship, love and support,
I thank you from the centre of my heart: Audrey Lewis Liz Mcknight, Kim Armati, Michelle Zhwar, Michelle Brown, Lisa Davies and Suzzie Cheetham. Without you ladies it would not have been possible to get through it all with ease and grace.

A big thanks to Sue and Aimee for the lovely photography and styling, and to my agent
Linda Williams who continues to see my vision in helping as many women around the world become healthier and happier.